JUST FRANK

JUST FRANK

*My Life as an
Intrepid Inventor*

Franklin G. Reick

FCP

*Full Court Press
Englewood Cliffs, New Jersey*

First Edition

Copyright © 2013 by Franklin G. Reick

Published in the United States of America
by Full Court Press, 601 Palisade Avenue
Englewood Cliffs, NJ 07632
www.fullcourtpressnj.com

ISBN 978-1-938812-12-5
Library of Congress Control No. 2013936355

Editing by Carol Karels

*Book Design by Barry Sheinkopf
for Bookshapers (www.bookshapers.com)*

Colophon by Liz Sedlack

To Florence

"It is not true that people stop pursuing their dreams because they grow old... They grow old because they stop pursuing their dreams."

—*Gabriel Garcia Marquez*

Foreword

THIRTY-SEVEN YEARS AGO I taught Frank Reick how to fly. It changed my life.

Learning to fly an airplane is no easy thing. Learning to safely cope with variables you have no control over is even harder: gusty cross-wind landings onto a short, muddy, grass strip with telephone wires at each end; simulated dead stick landings; and engine failure (actually I surreptitiously turned off the fuel.) It is during these tense moments— some simulated, some courtesy of Mother Nature— that you see the courage and spirit of a man. It may take months or years to discover a person's true character on the ground, but thousands of feet in the air, in a small cockpit, it only takes a few hours to determine their qualities of character and temperament. Frank was one of my favorites.

With serious enthusiasm, Frank immersed himself in the process. When it got too easy, I made it harder. Without breaking a sweat, Frank persisted and excelled, developing flying skills beyond that required by the FAA for a private pilot's license.

We worked hard, we had fun, Frank demonstrated his mettle, and we became friends.

At some point, the instructor/student relationship began to blur. Already a successful inventor, Frank began to coach me in the process of inventing. Nothing formal, just off-hand stories of his successes and failures. His intellectual stimulation gave my course heading a ninety-degree turn.

Thirty-seven years and twenty-five patents later, I'd say the student taught the instructor well. Thanks, Frank!

Al Kolvites,
Inventor/Retired Flight Instructor

INTRODUCTION

I WAS BORN TO be an inventor—an intrepid inventor. I've been disassembling and resurrecting things since I was three years old. I've taken apart everything from musical instruments to grandfather clocks; from electron microscopes to top-secret display generators. I've spent years of my life researching lubricants, superhydrophobic coatings, and how to grow diamonds. My first lab was two cinder blocks and a board under my parents' front porch in Poughkeepsie, New York. I've had numerous labs since then—in attics, basements, tree houses, garages and factories.

I'm also handy, and can make just about anything that's broken work again. I'm also the world's best scrounger. The saying, "What's one man's junk is another man's treasure" certainly applies to me! I'm on a first name basis with all the "gatekeepers" of the industrial junkyards in Newark. That's where most of the equipment in my factory came from. To me, all are valuable production machines. What gets me excited is resurrecting a pile of old pumps, blowers and compressors.

I also get excited about inventing newer and better products, and marketing them to the public. In my 82 years, I've been awarded forty patents; one is in the Guinness Book of World Records. I've also been a finalist for *Inc Magazine's* "Entrepreneur of the Year" award. I'm also a member of the New Jersey Inventors Hall of Fame. I'm still inventing and believe the best products are yet to come.

I'm often asked by business students, "What makes an inventor?" Even my patent attorney once said, "I'm a helluva lot smarter than you, Frank, so how come you're an inventor and I'm not?"

The Edison Innovation Foundation stated, "inventors are agents of change and great economic growth. They move the world in new directions and shift the paradigm." That description makes me think of famous inventors like Nicola Tesla, Henry Ford, Chester Carlson, Edwin Land and Steve Wozniak. Inventors, to my way of thinking, are those who see a need, try to improve an existing product, or accomplish the same goal in a radical new way. That's how thousands of products get invented every year, just by building a better mousetrap.

Some inventions are wildly successful; others dazzle like fireworks, then fizzle out. Some are duds from the get go. Most inventors are always on high alert for problems and opportunities, and are enthusiastic about challenging the entrenched way of doing things.

Inventors come in all types of packages but the ones I've spent time with are adventurous and fearless, have an active imagination and an insatiable curiosity. A vocabulary laced with expletives and a touch of madness also increase your chances of being a success, I've found.

Inventors Digest came up with their own list of the top ten traits of successful inventors:

1. *Persistence*
2. *Passion and intellectual curiosity*
3. *Independent minded, willingness to go against the grain*
4. *Ability to recognize and combine patterns into new ideas*
5. *Intuitive yet analytical with an ability to understand and interpret business data*
6. *Ability to 'sell' ideas and concepts*
7. *Focused on the future*
8. *Ability to draw on wide networks for perspective, advice and accomplishing tasks*
9. *Tolerance for risk and ambiguity*
10. *Willingness to fail and learn from failure*

Having good grades in school didn't make the list! That may be because it's often the class rebels, the students with dirt and grime under their nails, those who march to a different drummer, that become the inventors!

Besides personality traits, two other factors must be noted. First is having a *real* childhood, one with the freedom to explore, imagine, get dirty, create, succeed *and* fail. Future inventors need to learn life lessons, not just book lessons, in their childhood. The second is role models and mentors who help you put those life lessons in perspective.

Fortunately, I had both. Part One of this book is about my childhood and the role models who helped shape me into an inventor, as well as the object lessons I learned. Modern-day parents may be shocked at the stories I recall from my childhood, and at the freedom I was given from a young age, like Huckleberry Finn. Without that freedom, however, I wouldn't have made the mistakes, developed the confidence and curiosity, and learned the lessons that shaped me into the inventor I am.

Part Two is about my adult life as an inventor/entrepreneur and my advice to others who choose to follow the path of the inventor. In it I share both my triumphs and mistakes, and recollections of those who supported me on my exciting life journey as an inventor. While the support of family and close friends is important, of equal importance is a supportive government. By that, I mean the free market system that provides inventors like myself the freedom to dream, create, take risks, be a mild or wild success, or be a failure. It's a system that lets you start over and repeat the above cycle as often as desired. When government tampers with free markets by determining which products will be successful and which fail, whether through legislation or regulation, that's bad for inventors and for society in general.

PART ONE

ROWING UP, I WAS a 20th-century Huckleberry Finn. Due to my curiosity and fearlessness, I got into trouble, had some near fatal accidents, and almost accidentally crippled my father. Fortunately, I had role models and mentors who put these experiences in perspective. By the age of twenty, I'd learned dozens of object lessons that would shape my life as an inventor.

I was a boy who needed male role models to guide me through life. What boy doesn't? Girls need role models too, but boys need someone to provide a firm hand, a shoulder to lean on, challenging projects, and to teach us how to be good men. My father, Gerald Reick, was my first role model. Dad was a self-made man who never finished high school. Long before I was born, he learned how to engrave. He engraved the ID bracelets that were so popular among soldiers and teenagers during World War II. He also engraved rings and casket plates. Dad had a special set of tools that he used that included clamps, a rotating vice, rulers, wood, powder, and magnifying glasses. I was fascinated by the work he did, carving microscopic messages like "George loves Mary" on the inside of rings.

As I watched him at his craft, I realized what a gifted artist he was. Subsequently, I've had a great appreciation for the creative side of human beings. I've always sought out creative individuals and inventors as friends. I've always been humbled by brilliance. Most inventors are.

Dad was a frugal man who never wasted anything. It was the 1930s, during the Great Depression, and like most families, my parents did whatever they could to make ends meet.

One of my first memories of Dad was of him making elderberry wine and sauerkraut in the basement of our house on Fox Terrace in Poughkeepsie, New York. Dad would collect the elderberries on the side roads in the Wappinger's Creek area, then squash them and bottle the wine in the cellar. I was drawn by the marvelous berry smells wafting from the basement. Making my way down those steep stairs, one step at a time, was quite a challenge for a little guy. Making wine was an elaborate process and I never tired of watching him and being with him, smelling those wonderful aromas. I spent so much time in the basement with him that I thought our family was self-sufficient or in the food business. I wish I could say that I think of Dad every time I smell berries or sauerkraut, but after working in labs for more than six decades, my sense of smell is gone. I'd like to think that observing him in his "food lab" put me on the course of becoming an inventor.

Use Your Imagination

Winters in Poughkeepsie resulted in ice crystals on our windows. My mother called them "Jack Frost paintings." She'd always wake me excitedly and ask, "Look Franklin! What did Jack Frost paint in this window?" and encouraged me to use my imagination to discover magical, miraculous and exotic worlds in my window. Imagination is important. Cultivating one in your child is important. So is being in nature. It makes you aware of its power and beauty, and of finding balance in your life.

Cultivate a Competitive Spirit

Dad was a gentleman farmer. He had a green thumb and grew tomatoes and cucumbers so big they could make the *Guinness Book of World Records!* He was a competitive guy, and took great pride that his tomatoes were bigger and tastier than his neighbors, especially his good friend George Wolf. His secret might have been horse manure, because he'd often head over to the local horse stables with a bucket, and dig up old manure. Then he'd dig a hole about three feet wide by a foot-and-a-half deep in the field. He'd put a bit of the horse manure in the hole, top it off with soil, then plant seeds on top. The seedlings exploded out of the ground within days. Dad never mowed the field or pulled any weeds. With the exception of the cucumbers and tomatoes, the field was filled with wildflowers: Black-eyed Susans, daisies, and goldenrod, which, despite my severe allergies to them, I found them beautiful.

One of my late summer chores was picking the tomatoes and cucumbers. Some were half as big as I was, and if I wasn't careful, I could trip over them and sprain an ankle! We had so many tomatoes, I'd go from house to house with my little red wagon and sell baskets of them for fifty cents, well below the going rate at the time. I learned the value of respectful competition and marketing from helping Dad in the garden. Every inventor has a competitive nature, for we're always trying to improve on what's already out there. If our invention is unique and solves a problem, we also need to market and sell it, or hire a good PR and marketing firm to do that for us. If not, it's like the tree that falls in the woods. Nobody ever hears it.

Try to Improve the Status Quo

One time, Dad became obsessed with baked beans, and conducted a food experiment in the yard. We ate a lot of store-bought canned ones, and Dad thought they were all tasteless. So he decided to make them himself. With me at his side, he dug a hole in the side lot about one-and-a-half feet deep and several feet in diameter. He lined the bottom of the hole with lots of round rocks from the creek. He built a fire in the hole and allowed it to burn to ashes, thereby heating the rocks. In the meantime, he filled a ceramic crock pot with beans, pork cubes, pork fat chunks, molasses and brown sugar. After placing a lid on the pot, he placed it into the hole, then covered it with green straw and dirt. The mound steamed like a volcano.

Twenty-four hours later, he lifted the crock-pot out and brought it into the kitchen. The aroma coming out of that pot was as memorable as the elderberry wine and sauerkraut. The beans tasted good, but for all the work involved, they weren't a huge improvement over the canned ones. I think the experience was as much a ceremonial ritual as a cooking experiment. Dad never made baked beans again. He knew he could, but it was time to move on.

Like Dad, once I've solved a problem or developed a product to my satisfaction, I lose interest and move on. I consider myself a prosperous man for I love what I do, inventing in my laboratory, and that's what matters most to me.

Embrace Enthusiasm

I've never liked being around whiners, complainers, or pessimists. This goes back to my first day of kindergarten, which I remember being thrilled about. I was in school and so pleased that I was in the big leagues, about to embark on a new adventure in life. One of the boys in my class, Kenneth, carried on terribly after his mother left. He cried and cried, then threw up. He totally monopolized the teacher's time. The rest of us just had to sit and watch. His behavior disgusted me and put a damper on my enthusiasm for school. He was the first of many whiners and pessimists I've encountered in my eight decades. I do my best to avoid pessimists and naysayers who expend so much energy trying to dampen others enthusiasm and zest for life. I'm an optimist who loves life. I look forward to the adventures that every day brings. And I have confidence that every day will be fun and productive.

Be Confident and Curious

Both of my parents instilled confidence in me from a young age, saying I could accomplish anything I set my mind to. And for the most part, that's been true in my life. Besides confidence, they provided me with something every budding inventor needs: the ingredients to create a makeshift laboratory and junk to experiment with.

Our house had an entry porch with a semi-circular lattice shield under it. When I was five, I discovered I could prop it open and enter under the porch. Inside was a gigantic space to me, like the inside of a cathedral. It was there, at age five, that I created my first laboratory, after putting some boards across a few cinder blocks. I experimented on gadgets we picked up off the curb on trash day. Every gadget created by man fascinated me! I took apart old radios that had huge vacuum tubes, and old telephones with dials. My favorite discovery was an old wind-up gramophone with a crank on the side. It had a big horn on it with the trademark picture of the dog, "Little Nipper," listening to "his master's voice."

I was a curious boy, and *had* to take it apart. The inside was lubricated with primitive black grease, loaded with graphite, which got all over my hands, face and clothes as I worked. I was a little grease monkey and had great fun tinkering with all the springs and gears that made that gramophone run. I was oblivious to my appearance until my mother pointed out the greasy mess I'd left behind on the curtains and towels throughout the house. Making a mess is part of being an inventor, however, and had she forbidden my greasy childhood experiments, I might never have been a Guinness World Record inventor in later years with numerous patents and lubricants sold worldwide.

Express Awe and Joy

One of the most joyful childhood memories was the night Santa came to our home on Fox Terrace one Christmas Eve. I was five, and my mother had already tucked me into bed and said bedtime prayers with me. After I'd fallen asleep, she shook me awake, exclaiming, "Franklin, Franklin, you've got to come to the living room!" Out front, Santa Claus had his back to me and was placing presents under the tree!

"Go talk to him, Franklin," my mother urged. I tried to get Santa's attention by tugging at the back of his red suit. He turned around, and with a beaming smile, said "Ho, Ho, Ho Franklin! How are you?" Then he asked me to sing a Christmas song for him. After that, he chatted with me as if he'd known me my entire life—all five years! Santa Claus was in our house, he knew my name, *and* he was putting presents for me under our tree. I was jumping for joy.

After several minutes chatting with me, he said, "It's time for me to go, Franklin. You be a good boy all year and do what your mom and dad tell you." He went out the front door and I heard bells. He then shouted, "Ho, Ho, Ho" again and called out the reindeer's names. My mother restrained me from running outside to the front porch to say goodbye. "No, no Franklin. It's time to go back to bed." That was the only time in my life I met Santa Claus. I was so filled with awe and joy that it didn't even occur to me, despite my curious nature, that Santa was our neighbor and family friend Bob Adams. I love the Christmas spirit of "peace and goodwill to all." I wish they were more than just words, that all human beings treated each other this way.

Seek Freedom from the Mundane

Another childhood "laboratory" was the attic of our third home, on Lown Court, also in Poughkeepsie. My Dad had bought the house for the princely sum of three thousand dollars from the Crapser family. For many years, the house was heated by coal. One of my most dreaded chores was to help maintain the coal furnace, even though it was great fun to watch the coal truck dump the coal down a chute into the coal bin in our basement, and watch Dad shovel the new coal into the furnace. After that we'd have to light the coal, using paper, or wood. Whenever the fire went out, we had to restart it. What a pain!

At the bottom of the furnace was an ash grate, which

collected ashes, hot embers and clinkers (the pieces of coal that didn't burn). At least twice a week we had to shovel out the ash and remove the hot embers from the grate and put them in metal "ash" cans. The ashes were picked up twice a week and dumped in a local landfill. My dad finally got tired of all this and bought a stoker, a metal box with a screw in it that was automatically activated by a thermostat. It pushed the coal into the fire pit and eliminated most of the unpleasantness of my least favorite chore. To me, that stoker was one of the greatest inventions of all times! After that, all I had to do was keep the hopper full of coal.

Years later, we changed to oil heat, and didn't have to pay any attention at all. Dad wasn't an inventor, but he understood the value of those marvels and put them in place, making life easier for everyone. That's what inventions are all about, when it comes right down to it. They free us from mundane chores so we can be more creative and productive.

Build a Tree-House or a Field of Dreams

Every budding inventor needs a special place to think and dream—to let their imagination run wild. I had several as a child. My Dad was a fresh air fiend, perhaps over concern about the gaseous emissions from burning coal. No matter how cold it was outside, even in the dead of winter, he opened the windows at night, so by morning, the house was freezing! I'd grab my clothes, rush downstairs to the dining room, where the hot air coming out of the floor was the hottest, and place my clothes over the grate. Then I'd turn on the Zenith radio and listen to Fred Cook, a humorous talk show host, on WABC. Soon after, my parents would come down and, while Mom made breakfast, Dad and I would sit in the kitchen alcove and look out the window at our backyard. The yard had two garages with a shed between, and a row of mature sugar maple trees. Behind the yard was a vast field, the "playground" for me and my friends. For us, that undeveloped field was anything we young boys imagined it to be—a castle or a battleground. Years later, it became a baseball field.

My friends and I built a tree-house in one of the maples. We gathered all kinds of scrap in the neighborhood—wood, old rugs, and doors—to build it. We nailed a bunch of boards to the tree to create a primitive ladder. We'd spend half the day in our tree-house pondering the problems of the universe and coming up with ideas to solve them. While *we* used the trees as a leafy retreat from the adult world, one of our neighbors, Susan Ladue, made maple syrup from them. She nailed some long spikes into their trunks. From her we learned how to draw sap from the trees and evaporate the syrup over her stove.

Jump out of the Familiar Pond

I spent my childhood summers in a cabin that my Dad built, about 200 feet off Wappinger's Creek. A giant boulder, one that had been deposited by a glacier 10,000

years ago, sat in the middle of the creek. That same glacier left lots of gravel and smooth rocks behind on the
banks of the creek. My friends and I loved to sun ourselves on that boulder, dig in the gravel and throw skipper
stones across the creek. It was a magical, pristine place.

After Dad finished the house, he built a wooden dock.
My friends and I spent much of our summers swimming
and exploring the creek in the canoe, being little Huck
Finns.

Wappinger's Creek was teeming with small fish—
sunfish, crappies, rock bass, wide mouth bass, and pick-
erel. My friends and I caught them using worms, crickets
and grasshoppers for bait. We'd find the grasshoppers in
the fields, and the crickets under boards. We also caught
hellgrammites for bait. These larvae of the Dobsonfly,
also called "crawlerbottoms," congregated under rocks
below the dam. They were long black bugs with pincers
up front, a collar and lots of legs. We caught them behind
the head to avoid having our fingers caught in their pincers. When they bit, it hurt! But we caught a lot of fish
with them. We cleaned and scaled the fish and took them
home for our moms to cook. We considered the creek
part of our pantry, as the supply of fish seemed inex-
haustible.

The creek also had carp, and they were huge! We
rarely saw them, even when we swam and dove in the
creek, as they were bottom feeders. Occasionally, however, on a hot sunny day, they would often float up in
schools to sun themselves. They never bothered anybody.

We tried to catch them by putting dough balls and pieces of corn on a hook, but never caught any.

For some reason, the people who owned the adjacent country club wanted to rid the creek of the carp. They hired professional "carp catchers" who stretched a net across the creek by the dam and trolled upstream. I doubt they caught one carp in that net. What a waste of money!

The creek was lined with clumps of marginal plants that we called "spearheads" due to the shape of the leaf. Within each clump resided a large bullfrog. At sundown, they'd serenade us with their mating calls—a bellow that could be heard a half mile away. In the springtime, there'd be a background chorus of Spring Peepers, thousands of small frogs making high pitched calls to seek their mates. The frog chorus was hypnotic and we'd sit outside listening to the frogs instead of the radio.

One day Dad suggested we catch the frogs and eat frog legs. I had a wilderness survival book, one given to me by my Uncle Emory, that showed how to make snares and deadfall traps to catch small animals. That didn't interest me, but the chapter on catching bullfrogs did. All you needed was a fishing pole, six feet of line, and a fish hook baited with a one-inch pad of red cloth. We went out at night in the canoe with a flashlight and our pole and bait. We'd wiggle the red cloth near the frog; he thought it was a bug and gulped it. Using that technique, we caught a bunch of bullfrogs that Mother fried up for supper. They were delicious! A few nights later, I noticed the bullfrog chorus had stopped. I felt so ashamed. There was a seemingly endless supply of fish, but not bullfrogs. My friends and I created an ecological disaster before the term was even invented!

A quarter mile upstream was a bend in the creek where turtles sunned themselves. Catching turtles became a regular sport for us, but Dad didn't suggest we make turtle soup. We'd catch ten to fifteen of them, let them crawl around the canoe, then turn them loose near the house. Every turtle had unique markings, and after a while, we started noticing that we were catching the same turtles. My friend Jimmy Ladue got the idea that we should identify them, and glued little balsa wood sticks to their backs so they looked like submarines as they swam up the creek. It didn't take long for the glue to break loose, however, and we were back to catching the same turtles.

We then decided to paint a red mark on the turtle shells, and made a rule to never catch a red turtle. As the summer progressed, Wappinger's Creek became full of red-shelled turtles, and we no longer found it challenging to catch them. It was a life lesson for me. You don't learn much by hanging around the same pond, repeating what you already know. It's only by stretching your skills that you progress.

Confront a Bully

My friends and I would often play in the W. W. Smith School playground, which had teeter-totters, swings, a sandbox and a small wading pool. Nearby were a football field and a running track, as well as basketball and tennis courts. Most of the boys, including me, were scrappy kids and indulged in fist fights and wrestling to claim their place in the playground pecking order. Somebody always had a black eye. I had lots of respect for my friend Jack Ryan, who always won any jousting matches we engaged in and was higher than me on the pecking order.

I remember one little boy, Georgie, who was handicapped. He had a severe limp, and though he couldn't talk, he "chattered," making sounds none of us could understand. He always pulled a little wagon, all decked out with decorations, and just hung out in the playground watching us. Though Georgie was at the bottom of the pecking order, nobody bothered him.

But we had a classmate who was much heavier and taller than us who delighted in making *everyone* miserable on the playground. He was the classic playground bully. One day, after accepting our daily measure of abuse from him, my friend Jack had had enough, and punched the guy hard in the solar plexus. The bully doubled up in pain, out of breath. We all stared at him, jaws dropped, as he cried in agony. We were shocked that someone finally stood up to him. After that, he never bullied us again. That's when I realized bullies are cowards and will continue their taunting if unchecked. But firm retaliation will cure them of their aggression.

I wasn't bullied again until I was in my sixties, when my company was bullied by the State of New Jersey.

After a lifetime of being a relatively apolitical inventor, I remembered my friend Jack on the playground, and fought back. Since then, I maintain a constant vigil over any government action that bullies me, my fellow inventors, and small businesses. I lost track of Jack, but would like to thank him for his powerful object lesson.

Respect Your Elders

One of the highlights of my summer was the clambake held at the Poughkeepsie Country Club. Dad was one of the founders of the club. Back then it was a log building located just above the dam at Red Oaks Mill. Three men spent the day shucking oysters and clams, and I couldn't get enough of them! People even took bets on how many I could eat. Besides clams, there were all sorts of lawn games such as sack races, 3-legged races, and tug-of-war that I competed in. Inside the club were slot machines, then called One-Armed-Bandits. My parents gave me some nickels to gamble with, and I had a magic touch. Every time I put a nickel in, a flood of nickels poured out! I moved from machine to machine and had luck at each one. The thrill of winning, and the attention I received from the adults, was a high point of my childhood. I was a tycoon!

One of the members of the club was a *real* tycoon, and drove a Duesenberg convertible. He owned land near our house and built a huge fireplace out back. I worked alongside the stone mason and learned how to do stone work. The stone mason's name was Ernie Sweet and he got angry at me one day for calling him Ernie. "To you, kid, I'm Mr. Sweet." I was taken aback, but realized all he wanted was respect. From Mr. Sweet, I learned an important lesson in respect for your elders.

Appreciate Other Inventors

I was five when buses replaced the trolleys in Poughkeepsie. The trolleys fascinated me, with their probes picking up crackling electricity from an airborne wire and completing the circuit through the wheels. We'd ride the trolleys down Main Street to the Hudson River, to the historic ferry docks, where we could watch the boats and fishermen. I wish I could say the Hudson River was pristine during the Depression, but it was far from it! The water below the ferry docks was murky brown, and floating at the top were scraps of wood, bottles, cans, used condoms and human waste. It was a revolting cesspool, and it wasn't limited to the Poughkeepsie dock.

Poughkeepsie's drinking water also came from the Hudson River, albeit several miles north of the city. I had friends who used to swim in the river at Norry Point, north of the city. One told how he pushed fecal matter away as he swam. To make the water "safe" for drinking, it was pumped out of the river, put through a purification process, heavily chlorinated, then distributed through a vast network of pipes. The water tasted terrible! But we had no other options.

Back then, shad runs, the east coast version of salmon runs, were common in the spring. Thousands of these ocean fish swam upriver through all that crap, and laid their eggs north of Poughkeepsie. Shad fishing was big business then, and both amateur and professional fishermen came here with nets to catch shad. Every town on the river had Shad Festivals, and for weeks, everyone ate shad. My father loved shad roe, and devoured the fish eggs. He had no idea, at the time, that the roe was loaded with cholesterol. Is it possible that was what triggered the heart attack that would kill him at the young age of 44?

During those years, polio outbreaks were commonplace, and several of my grade school friends had become paralyzed from the disease, and wore steel braces on their legs. It was a nightmare for most parents because nobody really understood what caused it. Dirty air? Dirty water? The only treatments for severe cases were the "iron lung," which cost as much as a new house, or long periods of quarantine. Many parents, fearful and not knowing the cause of the disease, kept their children inside all summer. I'm so grateful my parents didn't do that. I needed to be outside, playing, making discoveries and having adventures. Being kept inside would be like an iron lung for me.

Polluted air and water, along with contaminated food, have been responsible for millions of untimely deaths in the past century. We should all be grateful to scientists and inventors like Dr. Jonas Salk and Dr. Albert Sabin who invented a vaccine, as well as all the engineer/inventors who pursue processes that make our food and water safe for the population.

Use Your Mind *and* Your Hands

My friends and I shared lots of adventures as kids, but one passion we didn't share was baseball. Our national pastime didn't excite me in the least, during the regular season *or* during the World Series. I couldn't understand why my friends were glued to the radio, listening to baseball day in and out. That's all they talked about. They memorized stats, recited scores, and filled their heads with trivia about the players. I found baseball, and the men who played it, boring as hell. Why fill your mind with all that crap, when you could be learning about the world and what makes it go round.

I was an information sponge by age seven. When my friends began to obsess about baseball, I became obsessed about how things work. I wanted to know everything. I was bored in school, I finished assignments quickly, and then I became a pest in class. Fortunately, my teachers told me, when things got slow in class, I could go to the library and read books that interested me. My parents weren't readers, but they did have a set of encyclopedias in the attic. When I was bored, I'd lay on the floor and read the encyclopedia, which I found fascinating; it transported me to a different world. I was a fast reader, thanks to our family friend Bob Adams, who had let me read newspapers and comic books in his cigar store, and I retained much of what I read. I learned more from independent reading than I did from classroom lectures. I want to know what's going on, to learn lessons from the past, and to create for the future.

Today, it seems that youngsters only read what is assigned in school. They're busy "texting," playing video games, and watching sports on television, which narrows their vision. Reading opens your mind to the world. Even sadder is that shop classes and auto repair classes have been discontinued from so many schools. Many boys who might be talented with their hands—future engineers, inventors, mechanics—never get the chance, in school, to discover this talent.

Focus on Freedom

I've been fascinated by airplanes and flying since I was about seven. For that reason, the Wright Brothers, who invented the airplane, are high on my list of favorite inventors. Poughkeepsie had several small airports in the 1930s. One was a big dirt field north of the city that small planes used to fly in and out of. A second airport, also a dirt field, was south of the city; it had a gigantic domed hangar. My friends and I loved hanging out and watching the planes land and take off. Years later, both airports were replaced by housing developments. A new airport, the Dutchess County Airport, was built when I was around eleven. My friends and I would watch the construction, mesmerized by the giant earth movers that radically changed the landscape.

Watching the planes fly in and out of those local airports was exhilarating and first got me thinking about freedom—freedom to fly like a bird and travel anywhere in the world. Those thoughts were the seeds that blossomed years later, after I got my pilot's license in 1971. I've now flown over 3700 hours. Flying my plane has been one of the great joys in my life.

Honor Nature

I've always been curious about landscapes and what they looked like before developed. Sometimes there are clues, other times not. There's a dam at Red Oaks Mill, on Wappinger Creek, which has always been a mystery to me. It's a big dam, about ten feet high and fifteen feet wide at the base, made of boulders and stones cemented together. Below the dam was a large spring with a galvanized pipe rammed into the wall. People came from all over with gallon bottles for that cool, clear water.

The water from the upper creek flowed over the dam, leaving an air gap between the falls and the stonework. When we were six or seven, my friends used to dare each other to cross the creek behind the falls. It was a sign of manliness at that age, yet the furthest we got was halfway across, where the water rose to our knees. Past the mid-point, it suddenly rose to our waists, and we'd scream and race back. Schools of rock bass hung out below the dam and we'd put crickets on a hook and pull out a fish almost every time. We'd take them home and eat them.

A swimming hole was just below the bridge. You could only get to it by climbing down a steep ravine. Ice cold springs ran down the pristine ravine, which was lined with thick moss, ferns and patches of watercress. During the spring and summer, the hill was covered with colorful flowers—dozens of varieties of iris in the spring, and daisies and purple spikes in the summer. It was magical, and how I imagined the Garden of Eden might look.

I searched through local history records to see when it was built and how it was constructed, but only found one photo, which depicted a nineteenth-century covered bridge with a mill just below, at the bend in the creek. The bridge has been rebuilt at least three times since that photo was taken, yet there are no written records.

With the exception of a small stand of yellow iris near the water, it's all gone now—the mill, the cold springs, the swimming hole, the moss, ferns, watercress, and the pipe. A strip mall was built atop the hill and the ravine is now full of trash—cans, bottles, broken glass, building material, and cinder blocks. I'm all for dreaming and building, but there's no excuse for mindless destruction.

Be Wary of the Cornered Rat

Our home on Lown Court, as I mentioned earlier, was built on cinder landfill and surrounded by undeveloped acres and vacant lots. Until it became developed, that land was used as a local dump for cinders, bottles, construction debris, and other solid waste. Fast-growing trees such as sumac and scrub brush blanketed the area. Like the nearby creek, it too was a Huck Finn paradise—lots of junk and easy to dig in.

Catching snakes with our bare hands was a favorite pastime. I discovered that garter snakes and milk snakes gathered under discarded sheets of corrugated roofing and old Nehi Soda signs. The snakes were easy to catch if you were quick and grabbed them just behind the head. A good size garter snake could get up to three feet long. I never got bit, but there were some close calls. At one time, I had about twenty-five snakes in a wooden crate and called myself the world's foremost expert on catching snakes. I always let them loose after a day or two.

One time I took a small garter snake to school in my pocket, and let it loose in class. Girls screamed, the teacher got flustered, and the janitor was called to catch it. Nobody ever knew it was me. I was a mischief maker! I was also fearless.

Wherever there's a dump, there are rats, and our neighborhood had lots! I spotted one climbing up one of the cinder block pillars that supported our back porch. I hooked up the garden hose, put it in the cinder block, and turned on the water at maximum force. Soon, a very wet and annoyed rat scrambled out and hovered in the corner of our porch steps. Since I was such an expert at catching snakes, I thought I'd try my hand at catching a rat. While trying to grab him, he dug his incisors into my left hand. Despite my pain and the blood spattering from my hand, I grabbed his tail and carried the angry thrashing rat inside the house.

Mother was serenely ironing on the kitchen's fold-down ironing board when I proudly exclaimed, "Mom, look what I caught!" She glanced up, saw the rat hanging below my bloody hand, turned pale and screamed, "Get that thing out of here!" I ran outside, baffled at my mom's response, and let the rat loose. Mother was in a state of panic. She called our family doctor, Dr. Crispell, who told her, "Get him to an Emergency Room as soon as possible."

At the hospital, I was the center of attention. One of the doctors said I needed a tetanus shot, and asked if I had any allergies. Mother told him I had a history of seasonal allergies and was allergic to strawberries. The tetanus shot at the time was made from horse serum, derived from the blood of purposely infected horses. Seconds after getting the injection, I went into shock. Apparently, I was allergic to horses! Some time later, I woke up in a hospital bed. My hand was wrapped in so much gauze it looked like a boxing mitt. *And* it smelled awful, like old urine! The treatment at the time for rat bites was a solution of urea. The bandages had to be soaked every hour in the stinky stuff, even after I'd gone back to school. Nobody wanted to come near me, the idiot who got chewed up by a rat.

The scars on my left hand are still visible—a constant reminder of my recklessness. The lesson I learned as a child was: cornered rats are dangerous and can kill you; leave it to the professionals to catch them. The lesson I learned as an adult is that rats in our society are not all four-legged, and encounters with them leave different types of scars. We'll get into that later.

Don't Be A Scoundrel

When I was eight, Jack Ryan and I were getting into mischief at the W. W. Smith Field. We figured out that the valves that controlled the sprinklers on the field were under a manhole cover, near one of the exits. We thought it would be great fun to turn on the valves. It was mischief making that wouldn't hurt anyone, we rationalized. The manhole cover was heavy, so we pried it up with a long screwdriver. Our goal was to lift it and move it out of the way, but Jack's hands slipped and the manhole crashed down on my right big toe.

I limped home, and told my parents. They didn't fuss about it, and never took me to the doctor, despite the pain I felt for the better part of a week. The resulting lump is still on my big toe! I'm convinced it broke and didn't heal properly.

It may seem like no big deal, to drop a manhole on your toe while engaging in a mischievous act, but the incident was a great life lesson and served me well all my life. I've read about too many bright, talented businessmen and politicians who have metaphorically dropped things on their toes, ruining others lives. The list of scoundrels who should have known better is long. Bernie Madoff, Bill Clinton, Richard Nixon, Jim Mc-Greevey, and Tiger Woods all come to mind. The lesson I learned early in life has kept me from becoming a scoundrel.

Respect the Power of Mother Nature

That same year, the Great Hurricane of 1938 hit our area. We were spending the summer in our cabin on Wappinger's Creek at the time. Outside, the wind sounded like a locomotive was passing by, and the rain came down in sheets. The creek rose and became a torrential river, grabbing everything in its path: fifty-gallon drums, a small gazebo, untethered row boats, and saplings. It wasn't long before the creek was six inches away from our front door! I thought it was the most excitement I'd ever experienced in my short life.

We fled the house, running through puddles that were morphing into lakes in our yard. We jumped in our Ford station wagon and headed toward the bridge that would take us to our home in Poughkeepsie. When we came to the bridge, water was running over the top of it. Mother was horrified; Dad was determined to get across the bridge before it collapsed or worse. He pulled the car back about fifty feet and slammed his foot on the accelerator. Our ancient Ford became an amphibious vessel and skimmed across the bridge at top speed. We made it to the other side. Mother was a nervous wreck for hours afterwards.

We made it home, and for the next week, Poughkeepsie was a "water wonderland" even Huck Finn would have loved. We made rafts and paddled down all the streets. After the water receded, we returned to our summer home to assess the damage. The water never did rise above the level it was at when we had fled. But all the bushes and trees had high water debris trapped against them. It was a great place for an eight-year old to explore. That disaster had created a great playground.

Thank Your Guardian Angels

I was in third grade when the great ice storm struck. Huge icicles hung from the power lines, telephone poles and eaves of every house. Everything was covered with ice! For a week, Poughkeepsie became a spectacular crystal wonderland, the likes of which I haven't seen since. Telephone poles and wires were down, the power was out, and school was closed. Kids loved it. My best friend Dick Rose and I put on our racing skates, and skated as fast as we could on the frozen creek that led to the Hudson River, and under the bridges. We were terrors on skates, and had a marvelous time exploring all the frozen areas of Poughkeepsie on skates after that storm. Toward the end of the week, as the temperature rose, we skated on Wappinger's Creek and came upon clear ice. *Danger!* That meant the ice was too thin. We skated like mad and the crack followed close behind. If we had stopped, we would have fallen through the ice. The guardian angel of adventurous boys looked out for us.

Paddle Together
In the Right Direction for Best Results

I learned a lesson about teamwork after a bunch of us went canoeing above the dam. It was me, the two Cundy brothers, and Jimmy Ladue, whose leg was in a cast. He was in the back of the boat steering. The water was low, but the current was strong. Jimmy noticed a log that was hung up on the dam and thought we should give it a push. Jimmy started paddling toward the dam. The rest of us protested and paddled the opposite direction, but the current grabbed us, and our boat went nose first over the dam onto the slate rocks below. The nose of the boat crumbled like an accordion. Nobody got hurt, but as we sat on the rocks below the dam, we could see Jimmy's cast was soaked. I was crying, upset because I felt certain my Dad would kill me. After we calmed down, we dragged the boat back up to the cabin. Dad was there, and much to my surprise, he didn't even raise his voice. He seemed relieved that we were all in one piece. Then he turned his attention to the canoe, and we realized it could be salvaged. I got out my tools, boards, glue, nails, slats, paint and a canvas patch and we set out to fix it. It wasn't perfect, but it floated. My source of summer freedom was restored! What I learned from that adventure was the importance of teamwork. People have to paddle in the same direction to get good results.

Choose Your Friends Wisely

Remember the movie *A Christmas Story,* by Jean Shepherd? It was about nine-year-old Ralphie Parker, who begged his parents for a Red Ryder BB gun. Every kid had one when I was growing up. We took them everywhere we went, mostly to shoot bottles. One summer day, my friend Jimmy and I paddled up the creek in my canoe. That day, Jimmy brought along a friend named Smitty, a big guy who towered over us. He didn't talk much, and I didn't like him. We pulled ashore near a pump house. Smitty grabbed Jimmy's BB gun and proceeded to shoot out the windows of the pump house. Jimmy and I yelled at him and tried to make him stop. But he was tough and big, and prevailed. We jumped in the canoe and paddled back silently. Jimmy and I were worried sick, knowing we were witnesses to a crime. Smitty seemed proud of his wanton destruction.

Two days later, the sheriff pulled up in our driveway looking for "two boys with BB guns." Jimmy and I were in the front yard and confessed. He told us to give him our guns; we told him we couldn't find them. (We had buried them by the creek shortly after our crime.) He said he wanted to speak with our parents. I was terrified. Even though I hadn't shot the windows, I knew we were in big trouble. Our parents made peace by offering to replace the windows. Jimmy and I would measure the windows, our parents would have the glass cut, and Jimmy and I had to install them.

When it came time to install the glass, we realized Jimmy hadn't measured the windows correctly, and all the panes of glass were a hair too large for the frames. We did the best we could. We cleaned out all the broken glass and then installed the windows the way young boys who were clueless about window replacement would. It was a God-awful sight when we finished with cock-eyed windows and putty everywhere. We paddled back home and didn't hear anything from the owners. Later, when we paddled by, just to see if the windows had survived, we noticed the windows had been corrected. I guess the owners decided we'd learned our lesson. For me, the lesson was to not hang around with people who destroy property, flee the scene, and leave it to others to clean up. Since then, I carefully choose my friends and associates.

Don't Point A Gun At Something You Don't Want to Kill

When I turned twelve, Dad got me a .22 long rifle. It was a "rite of passage" gun, one used for recreational shooting and small-game hunting. The difference between a BB gun and a .22 rifle was that the rifle was a lethal weapon. You could lose an eye with a BB gun, but not your life. Dad would take me up to a bend in the creek above our summer home where there was a slate outcropping to practice. Or we'd go to the nearby quarry. He taught me how to hold the gun and how to load it. The magazine had a six-bullet clip and once loaded, he taught me to aim, hold the rifle steady, "hold your breath," and squeeze the trigger slowly. I practiced on bottles he'd throw into the air. We found most of the bottles in a nearby dump, where truckloads of bottles had been dumped in past years. In no time, I felt like a "can't miss" rifleman out of the Old West. We did nature a great service by blasting those bottles into smithereens, hastening their return to sand. Dad was an outstanding teacher, and I became an excellent marksman.

I put my marksman skills to use when woodchucks ravaged my Dad's garden, even after he put up a rabbit fence. After finding half his tomatoes, string beans and carrots missing, Dad ordered me to "Shoot the God-damned things and bring them home for dinner." I shot two, and took them to George Wolf, the local game warden. He showed me how to skin them. "Be careful you don't puncture the musk glands under their front and rear legs," he warned me. "The fluid is pungent and tastes awful." I took them home to Mother, who quartered them, soaked them in salt water for a day, cooked them in a pressure cooker, then baked them with sauce in the oven. It seemed like a lot of work, but they were tasty. Dad ate them with gusto, as if he was getting even with them for causing havoc in his garden.

Two lessons about owning a gun have stayed with me for seven decades: "Franklin, never point a gun at something you don't plan to kill," and "There's no such thing as an unloaded gun." Although I was raised with guns, I don't own one.

Recklessness Has Consequences

In 1942, in the midst of World War II, the father of one of my buddies worked at a plant making magnesium parts for airplanes. Magnesium is lighter than aluminum and more reactive. He got me some scrap samples and I ground it into a powder with a grinding wheel. Wooden "strike anywhere" matches were common at the time. I cut the heads off a dozen or so, carefully crushing them with a pair of pliers so they wouldn't ignite. I then mixed them with the magnesium, an incredibly dangerous concoction. We placed a small pile of the powder/matchhead mix on the sidewalk and hit it with a hammer. It ignited with a brilliant white blinding flame and melted a hole in the concrete. It was the stuff incendiary bombs were made of. Once lit, it couldn't be extinguished; steel would melt as easily as concrete. I stored my powder in an empty coffee can, in the attic, unlabelled. I went to visit a friend for a few days and came back to find Dad's right hand wrapped in a bandage. I learned he'd been working in the attic and snuffed out his cigarette in the can. The result was a third-degree burn on his engraving hand. I was horrified at what I'd done. If there had been more of that concoction in the can, it would have taken his hand off.

The worst part was that Dad didn't yell at me or express anger. I suppose he knew me well enough to know that my understanding of what happened, and what might have happened, was punishment enough. His burns healed quickly, and he went back to engraving. I was greatly humbled by the experience. Recklessness has consequences. Catching wild rats, playing with duds, leaving boards with nails in them and not labeling cans with dangerous substances... All were reckless acts that could have killed someone.

Don't Mess with Duds!

The Fourth of July was always a great adventure for the kids in Poughkeepsie. Fireworks were legal in New York then, and Poughkeepsie more resembled the invasion of Iwo Jima than a small river town at night. All hell broke loose after the sun set, as firecrackers, cherry bombs, Roman candles and bottle rockets made thunderous noises and lit up the night sky with a mosaic of colors.

Buying the fireworks was as much an adventure as setting them off. Dad took me to a grocery store that stocked up on them in June. We'd drive down a bumpy, two-lane gravel road alongside the creek to get there. The store was packed with every flashy type of pyrotechnic imaginable at the time: rockets, big bangers, cherry bombs and fire fountains.

A couple of dollars would get you some cherry bombs, a handful of small firecrackers, and a couple of six-inchers—small sticks of dynamite. Dad always got some bottle rockets and Roman candles. Once home, we'd unwind all the firecracker strings. Then my friends would come over with the fireworks they'd bought and we set off the smaller firecrackers and toss them into the woods. We put the larger ones under cans, lit the fuse and ran, then watched the can shoot 20-30 feet in the air. We tied cherry bombs to rocks and threw them in the creek. They went off like depth chargers.

Sometimes, we'd light the fuse and nothing happened. *Duds!* We'd break the duds in half so we had two halves latched together by a hinge of paper. We'd then stick a wooden match into the powder, ignite it and watch it take off. *Sizzlers!* They'd spin around in circles.

Dad always warned us against messing with duds, and I didn't take him seriously until after I burned my left hand trying to light one. The blisters on my hand lasted several days, and hurt like hell! They provided the lesson my father couldn't. *Don't mess with duds!* It's amazing I didn't blow off my hands and fingers. Lots of kids did every Fourth of July. As a result, the town outlawed fireworks. Now we have to watch others shoot them off. It's a lot more fun shooting them off yourself. Childhood adventures are important learning experiences, but you need to combine them with common sense.

Never Stop Thanking Your Guardian Angels

Dad was a frugal gentleman farmer. During World War II he got ticked off because the price of eggs had gone to a dollar a dozen. He didn't approve of egg price inflation, so he decided to raise his own chickens. He built an incubator of sorts in the basement of his jewelry store, bought a dozen fertile eggs, and gently placed them in the incubator. Just for fun, he bought some duck eggs too. Every day we'd go down and check on them.

One day, I noticed that one of the eggs was rocking back and forth and there was a hole in it. A yellow, fuzzball chick emerged about an hour later. Soon, a dozen little chicks were running around the basement. We gave them water and fed them mash. Chickens and ducks get imprinted by the first big animal they see, so we became their "parents."

Dad's next project was to build a chicken coop out by the creek. Times were tough, and Dad got the lumber from a salvage yard on Route 9W. The back of the station wagon was filled with used boards that had been ripped off the side of a demolished building. The boards still had nails protruding from them.

I was given the job of pulling out the nails, straightening them, and saving them. Dad insisted on reusing everything. Nothing ever went to waste! Once Dad had enough wood, I stopped pulling out the nails. He drove some stakes into the ground and built an 8' x 8' chicken coop with a slant roof over it. It had a ramp for the chickens to run up and down, a yard for them to walk and scratch, and a roost for them to sleep and lay eggs. He also built a door for us to go in and out, and wrapped chicken wire all around. The chickens and ducks were happy with their new home. We fed them mash, installed a water fountain, and threw cracked corn as a treat.

The cracked corn attracted all the river rats, who travelled all over from the creek. I often caught those rats feasting on the corn as the chickens cowered in their roost. That's when my skills with my .22 rifle came in handy. The only animals I ever took pot shots at were those rats. As good a marksman as I was, I rarely hit them. The rats were smart and stayed away when they saw me with my gun. Then I put a scarecrow with a stick on top of the coop, but they eventually got wise to that as well. Rats, I learned, were super smart! I'd then sit on the roof and try to pick them off. I managed to get a few, but realized it was impossible to rid the place of them.

One day, I jumped off the roof of the chicken coop

and felt instant pain in my left foot. I looked down and there was a nail coming through the top of my shoe. I was impaled on one of the boards that still had nails in it! My first thought was, "What am I going to tell my parents?" And my second was, "I can't go to the hospital!" *They almost killed me with a tetanus shot the last time I went!* I placed my good foot on the board and pulled the other foot free. My foot didn't bleed, but the pain was intense, and throbbing. I never told my parents because I didn't want them to make a big fuss about it. Much to my amazement, my foot didn't get infected and I didn't die of tetanus. I'm very grateful. The guardian angel of adventurous boys often worked overtime with me.

Respect Boundaries

My whole family became very attached to our chickens and ducks, which we considered pets. Dad ran a chicken wire fence from our house to the creek so they could run freely, safe from predators. The white ducks had a marvelous time with their new-found freedom, and loved splashing in the creek. Two of the ducks became very attached to Mother. We named them Donald and Dopey. Mother came out several times a day and hand-fed them, which made them even more attached to her. They often waddled up to the front door and quacked until she came out to feed them. They were very demanding, but everyone loved them. While the other ducks had to stay within the fence, Donald and Dopey had free reign of the yard. They waddled around, followed people, and nibbled at visitors. They "owned" the place.

One night, we heard a big fuss in the yard. We discovered that our neighbor's dog wandered into our yard and killed our pet ducks. Mother was heartbroken and took it personally. Two members of her family had been killed by a dog that should have been controlled by its owner. There was great tension between our two families for a while. Their dog had violated our family's "space" and destroyed our property. I believe this is why I'm a strong advocate for property rights and all that entails in our society. Respect for the property of others leads to harmonious relationships. Disrespect leads to conflict.

Honor the Food You Eat, Whether it's a Chicken...

Eventually Dad built a second chicken coop, one for the Bard Rocks and the other for the Rhode Island Reds. Many of my chores revolved around the chickens. I had to feed them, collect the eggs from the nests, and sell the eggs. We got quite a few eggs, and I'd sell them to our neighbors.

In some ways, those chickens were like pets. I'd collect sorrel, a sour grass, in the fields and bring it as a treat for them. When they saw me coming with a handful of sorrel, they'd go crazy and devour it. To them, it was like ice cream to kids. There was one hen at the bottom of the pecking order. Mother brought her into the house and hand fed her until she became quite tame. We turned her loose in the yard, but whenever Mother called her,

"Chick, chick, chick," she'd come racing to the door to get her neck scratched.

Another chore was cleaning the chicken coop. We used the chicken manure to fertilize our garden. Removing the poop from the coop was a distasteful chore, but killing the chickens was the worst. Most kids that grow up on farms do this all the time. But we lived in a town. Dad, as I've mentioned, was a survivalist, so growing our own food was part of our lives.

I dreaded every time Mother would say, "Franklin, we're going to have chicken tomorrow. Go kill a chicken."

Our family friend Bob Adams taught me how to do this. He set up a saw horse with two nails partially driven in two inches apart. First, I had to catch the bird. He told me to always select a rooster, since they were noisy, didn't lay eggs and pestered the hens. The roosters were smart enough to know what was coming, and always gave a good chase. Then I'd hold it by its feet and swirl it hard to knock him out. I'd then put the head between the two nails, stretch his neck, and lop off the head with an axe. The headless bird would race around the yard spewing blood until it finally fell down. I then dipped the carcass into boiling hot water, and plucked out the feathers. Finally, I slit the bird open and removed the guts. It was a lot of work, all unpleasant!

If you find this repulsive, as I did, the next time you eat a chicken, or any animal, remember that somebody had to look it in the eyes before they killed it, cleaned it and prepared it.

When somebody else does your killing for you, it's not any easier on the chicken.

...Or a Pig

One of Dad's closest friends was George Wolf. George had a home below the Wappinger's Creek dam, and owned a sporting goods store in Poughkeepsie. Like Dad, George was a gentleman farmer and as competitive as Dad. Each summer they had a competition about who could grow the best tomatoes. Dad's were always bigger and tastier.

One summer they decided to get piglets. Since George had more space in his yard, they built a pigpen on his property. The baby pigs were cute and lovable, and our mothers dubbed them "George" and "Gerry." We kids fed the pigs, talked to them, scratched them on the back of their heads between their ears. It wasn't long before the pigs were bigger than me! I felt bad for them, confined in a relatively small pen which resembled a muck heap.

One day the pigs escaped. They were just as happy as two grown pigs can be, running alongside the creek, wagging their curly tails, snorting in glee. We kids were assigned the task of catching them, and we soon learned that catching a newly freed pig is a very difficult job, especially for a kid my size. Soon we became a gang rushing around and chasing them. George and Gerry did everything they could to avoid their mucky pen, and as big as they were, they were fast! I'm not sure how we finally caught them. Perhaps we just wore them out. But back to their miserable pigpen existence they went. By the end of the summer, they were huge.

George and Gerry were taken to the butcher in the fall. We kids had never been told this would be their fate. One day they were wallowing in their pigpen, the next they were returned to us as a pile of sausage and ham hocks. The salted ham hocks were hung up in the basement. Dad said they'd get better with age.

The sausage was the best I've ever eaten in my life. Poor George! Poor Gerry! It seemed like cannibalism to eat an animal that was part of the family, but that's the way things were growing up in the Depression. You grew your food—whether it was tomatoes or ham and sausage.

If You're Going to Build Something, Plan Ahead

Bob Adams, like everyone else who lived along Wappinger's Creek, had a boat. Also on Bob's property was a rusted-out Model T Ford truck. It had all kinds of mysterious parts. My friends and I pretended it was a getaway car, even though all the tires were flat. We'd imagine the cops chasing us, we'd shoot at them, and we'd get shot. It was a magical place for boys with overactive imaginations. Some of the modern toys don't leave room for imagination. Imagination is essential for a budding inventor.

Bob's property acreage from the creek was spectacular, with a cove, all sorts of flowering marginal plants such as purple loosestrife and white water lilies. Red-winged blackbirds nested in the plants and turtles sat on the logs. Spending my summers there gave me a lifelong appreciation for the wonder of nature.

When I was nine, Bob Adams built a house along the dirt road behind our summer home. He let me be his assistant while he built his house. From him I learned how to do BX wiring at a young age. I also heard classical music for the first time in his house. He had a big wooden Crosley radio, and I was stopped in my tracks by the beautiful music that came out of it. He told me it was Franz Schubert's *Trout Quintet*. I'd never heard of Franz Schubert or his *Trout Quintet*, but I stood mesmerized, listening until it was over.

Bob was an oddball, and like Dad, was also on a survivalist kick. After building his house, he said he needed a cold cellar to store roots, cabbage, carrots and potatoes during the winter. He blasted a hole in the side of the hill, and built the cellar with slate sides, a domed concrete roof, and a door. I watched him and helped whenever he asked.

He then decided he wanted a basement under his house. His house was built on slate, so this was no easy process. He hired some half-baked day laborers to help him dig a trench on the creek side of the house. It was a tedious process and Bob lost patience with the workers. Another neighbor, Mr. Perkins, was a contractor who lived in a log home. He suggested they dynamite the stone from under the house. I got to watch as they dragged in big wire cable nets and put them between the slate air gap and the house, then proceeded to blast. The blast tore away about a third of the area. By then, Bob was tired of that project, and told us he was going to make a violin. He found some wood and began shaving the various parts. I had no idea he could carve, yet it appeared very elegant.

Bob was like that, going from one project to an entirely unrelated one. Although he was an oddball, he had a great influence on my life. I learned a great deal from watching him work. Perhaps the most useful thing I learned was that if you're going to build something, you need to plan ahead. You don't dig trenches or basements underneath houses built on rock. Bob came from a different school of thought. He didn't think planning ahead was necessary. Perhaps he should have gone into politics.

You Get What You Pay For

Dad's jewelry business was doing well, so he purchased a parcel of land about a mile west of the the Red Oaks Mill area. Apparently he'd gotten a good deal on the property, which had five acres of open farmland and ten acres of pine forest. He had the open area plowed and then planted soybeans. Soybean roots, he said, carried nitrogen-fixing bacteria that would improve the soil. The wooded area had hills and gullies, "Tarzan vines," and a swampy area that was home to black snakes, newts and peepers. Deer, squirrels and other mammals also populated the forest. Somebody had once lived there, as we discovered an old stone foundation and a stone well that teemed with mosquito larvae. If not for the swarms of mosquitoes, gnats and horseflies, it would have been a great place for me and my friends to hang out in the summer.

Dad hired a father and son team to help him build a barn near the woods. He must not have paid them much, for it quickly became clear that they had no idea what they were doing. They constantly cursed at one another as they sloppily poured concrete footings and laid the cement blocks for the walls. They then built a roof of rough-sawed timbers. The final step was pouring the concrete for the floor. The wet cement was mixed in a Spoor-Lasher Ready-Mix concrete truck, then released down a slide. Our hired hands weren't up to screeding and smoothing the concrete. Dad panicked, realizing that the concrete might set before it was smoothed out. He raced into town, and hired two professionals at a premium hourly rate, who saved the day. After building a loft, we finally had a crude barn. Dad was ecstatic.

Celebrate Success

Poughkeepsie was a magical place after it snowed. Christmas Eve in 1942 was right out of a Norman Rockwell painting. Fresh snow had fallen, and families were trudging through the snow to complete their Christmas shopping. Christmas music wafted through loudspeakers downtown. Dad's jewelry store was packed and he worked late. I had already fallen asleep for the night when Dad came into my bedroom, shook me awake, and exclaimed, "Franklin, look at this!"

He had a wad of bills in his hand. "Three thousand dollars, Franklin! That's what we did in the store today!" He wanted to share his success with me. I was only twelve and had no idea of the struggle it was for him to start a business during the Depression and and support our family. I said, "That's great, Dad," and fell back to sleep.

Don't Take Life for Granted

Less than two years later, my father died from a heart attack, at the age of 44, when I was fourteen. Mother had found him in the bedroom, sputtering, twitching, and gurgling. She yelled for me, "Franklin, Franklin, something's wrong with your father!" I ran into the room and grabbed his hand, but he wasn't able to communicate with me. His eyes rolled back, he heaved a big sigh, and that was it. My father was dead. No last words for me, no goodbyes, no closure. It was all so sudden, so traumatic, and unbelievable. My father, who was so close to me, was gone.

The next few days—the wake and the funeral—were like a blur to me. People from all over Poughkeepsie came to our house to view Dad in the coffin. Every corner of the house was filled with flowers, and mourners. I faded into a trance as friends and acquaintances of his approached me, shook my hand, and told me how sorry they were. Dad's best friend, Mr. Wolf, broke down and sobbed. Dad's friend Bob Adams offered to take me on a drive, just to get me out of the house. He did his best to cheer me up, and offered me a cigarette. "It's okay, Frank," he said, so I did.

His funeral was packed with people. Most of them drove out to the cemetery too. I couldn't watch as they lowered the casket into the ground. I ran to a nearby hill and sobbed for hours. I grieved for days and months.

Reach Out and Help Someone

Immediately after Dad's death, Bob Adams, who we all called "Uncle Bob," took me under his wing. Uncle Bob had owned Adams Cigar Store on Main Street, on the corner near Dad's jewelry store. When I was younger, he gave me "library privileges" at his store, and let me read any newspapers and comic books. On Sunday, he'd let me read "the funnies." We couldn't afford newspapers at home, so this was always a treat, since I loved to read anything I could get my hands on. Having access to all the newspapers and magazines in his store inspired me to become an avid reader.

Uncle Bob had also supplied me with junk he found— typically broken machines. To me they were treasures that I loved to take apart, marvel at the mechanisms in-side such as balls and pistons, and put them back together. One day, when I was about eight, he gave me a bass fid-dle he'd found. It was bigger than I was! I had to take it home to show my mother, who got a laugh when she looked out the window and saw this bass fiddle with a pair of legs on either side coming down the hill. I stored it in my laboratory under our front porch, and it became one of my treasures.

After Dad's death, Uncle Bob also helped Mother run the jewelry store for a few years. By then, he had closed his cigar store. I'd sit at the repair bench with him, as I had with Dad, and he'd teach me how to resize rings and fix broken bracelets, tell me stories, and draw pictures of a perpetual motion machine he was inventing. I also hung out with the two watchmakers, Mr. Vignes and Mr. Nielsen. It was like a men's club; they did their best to help me get through my loss.

Adults don't often realize what a difference they can make in the life of a teen, whether it's giving words of encouragement or calling them out on bad behavior. As a child, I was curious, bright, and fearless. As a teen, I was a top student, but I was easily bored, a smart ass, and a rebel. I was a challenge even to teachers for whom I had great respect.

I could easily have self-destructed if it wasn't for several men who took a fatherly interest in me at critical stages in my life—in high school, college and the business world. All these men carried on where my father had left off. They helped me create an interesting life and become a productive member of society. They taught me perseverance despite setbacks, whether personal or in business. They taught me life lessons that I never forgot. And they expected great things from me. That, perhaps, was the most important thing of all.

Expect Greatness

When I was fifteen, I took a radio course, which was great fun. I had read an article in *Popular Science* magazine about how to build a superheterodyne receiver. I had a list of parts, and managed to find all of them at a radio parts store on lower Main Street in Poughkeepsie. At home, I bent some sheet metal for a frame, and punched holes in it for the tubes and sockets. I had such a great time following the circuit diagram in the magazine, wiring it all together. When I needed help, one of our local radio repairmen discovered I had the wrong coil in one spot. I was mesmerized and spent hours in the evening tuning into various stations, and marveling that my concoction worked. I took it to school to show my Physics teacher Mr. Archibald. After inspecting it, he said, "Franklin, I've never known anyone to do anything like that!" That was one of the greatest compliments in my young life.

I was fascinated by science and math, and did well in both subjects, even though I wasn't always on my best behavior. Even so, I knew Mr. Archibald expected me to do my best. I remember taking a Physics exam that I finished earlier than everyone else. I wasn't quite sure of one answer, and looked over the shoulder of the guy ahead of me. He wasn't a great student, so it made no sense for me to do that. My eyes caught those of Mr. Archibald. He winced and looked away, betrayed, in a way, by his star student. We both knew I didn't need to cheat for an answer. I've never forgotten the look on his face. He never said anything. His eyes said it all. He expected more from me.

Another teacher who expected greatness of me was Mr. Bigelow, my Advanced Algebra teacher. He was tall and skinny, and resembled the character Ichabod Crane from the book *Tales of Sleepy Hollow*. He would unconsciously pick his nose in class, and we kids called him "Booger Bigelow" behind his back. He was an excellent teacher, and I was one of his better students, but smartass that I was, I did my best to annoy him. I often came to his class with a cigarette behind my ear. Back then, cigarettes were "good for you" and ads showed doctors in white coats encouraging you to smoke. Every kid in high school was smoking—it was a rite of passage, but I could tell it upset Mr. Bigelow.

Once, I pretended to read a paperback novel while he lectured. I knew he was watching me, and that he was bothered by my devilish behavior. He should have said something like "Cut the crap, Franklin," but he didn't.

Mr. Bigelow took great pride when his students did well on the end-of-year Regents exams, and we both assumed I'd aced the test. I finished before everyone else, turned in my exam, and left the exam room. Seconds after walking out the door, I realized I'd made a mistake on one of the questions. But it was too late. A few days later, while going from one class to the next, I passed the teacher's lounge and caught Mr. Bigelow's eye. He stormed into the hall and, looking like the Angel of Death, pointed a condemning finger at me.

"You!" he exclaimed. He was clearly furious at me because I'd only gotten a 99 on the Algebra Regents exam, not 100. I'd let him down. Thinking back, he was a great man. I wish I had the chance to thank him while he was still alive, for not accepting anything less than I was capable of.

Another teacher who accepted nothing less than my best was Mr. Hawkins, our high school band director, who encouraged me to play the trumpet in the high school band. I had developed an interest in music, specifically the trumpet, when I was ten. I wanted to be just like Harry James. Dad promised he'd buy me a trumpet if I practiced every day, and like every child, I promised. A friend of my father, Max Arnold, had been a trumpet player in John Philip Sousa's band, and offered to teach me for $2 an hour. Once a week, he came to our house for a lesson. He'd play a selection from the exercise book, and then we'd play together. He'd grade me each week, and after hearing, "Franklin, I can see you didn't practice much last week" for weeks on end, I finally put my nose to the grindstone and practiced regularly.

The practice paid off. In high school, I practiced several hours a day, including forty-five minutes of lip exercises. My goal was to beat Maynard Ferguson in the high ranges. It wasn't long before I became first chair in the trumpet section, and I later became President of the band. Mr. Hawkins became a trusted advisor and surrogate father to me. He set me straight when I needed it. He taught us how to march on the football field, and perform halftime routines.

I also was selected, by the Commander of the local American Legion, to play Taps at the funerals of local soldiers who had perished in World War II. Whenever there was a funeral, the VFW commander picked me up at school and drove me to the cemetery. I put my heart and soul into playing Taps for those who had given their lives for our country, most not much older than me. It was the least I could do.

After I graduated from high school, I could easily have pursued a career as a musician. Big bands were all the rage, and I was offered a job as a trumpet player in Ray Eberle's big band. He had been a vocalist in Glenn Miller's band, so it was quite an honor to be asked.

Mother would have none of it. "You're going to college!" she insisted. I'm grateful she did, and I headed off to Syracuse University with trumpet in hand. It didn't take long, however, for me to realize I was greatly outclassed by the music majors at Syracuse. And after some "death threats" by some seniors who got sick of hearing my relentless practice, I realized academics, not music, had to be my top priority in college. I dropped the trumpet and haven't played it since. You have to know when to fold your cards.

Dive Into Life

One of my favorite books as a teen was Jules Verne's 20,000 *Leagues Under the Sea*. I was fascinated by the undersea world, and had read the book five or six times.

One day, when I was fifteen and walking home from school, I spotted an old hot water boiler in a junkyard. What *I* saw was a diving helmet, and I took it home to my attic lab. Using chalk, I outlined where to cut for shoulders, face plate and a hole for the air line. Mr. Welde, a welder who had been friends with my father, offered to cut out the shape for a nominal fee. I ground the edges smooth, hammered out a chest plate and frame for a window cut from a sheet of steel. Mr. Welde brazed them together for me for $17.

I painted it black with a plexiglass face plate. A garden hose supplied air from two bicycle pumps on the surface. When I put it in water, it floated like a cork, not what I'd thought. Bob Adams found some lead for me. We melted it and poured it between the chest plate and helmet until it was heavy enough to sink and hold me on the bottom. My friends and I had a great time that summer exploring the bottom of lakes and creeks around Poughkeepsie.

My interest in underwater exploration continued at Syracuse. Syracuse Surplus was a jewel of a junkyard. Rodd Phibbs, a fraternity brother, and I found a pile of WWII stainless steel oxygen tanks. Jacques Cousteau had recently introduced scuba gear with his book, *The Silent World*. Let me tell you, it's far from silent down there. We fitted out a tank with a quarter-turn valve run with an automobile choke cable. If you wanted air, you gave a quick push and the cable would open it for you. It was a true demand regulator. Just as with my earlier diving helmet, if floated like a cork. We ended up wrapping it with iron sash weights we'd also found in the junkyard. It was heavy as hell, but fine when in the water. We filled it with air at the gas station. It's a wonder my lungs are still working! At age sixty, I got a PADI license so I could explore the reefs and underwater creatures off the coast of Florida and in the Caribbean.

Do *Different* Work

I spent my first year at Syracuse University as a Business Administration major largely due to Mother's influence. She had been running Reick's Jewelry Store since Dad's death. Unfortunately she wasn't a good manager nor did she have good business sense, so she expected me to take it over after I graduated from college. But I was bored silly in those economics and accounting classes. I could barely keep my eyes open in class or while reading the textbooks. I loved science and math, and my natural predilection was to build radios and diving gear, to take apart junk and repair car engines, *not* run a jewelry store.

I rebelled against my Mother and didn't work in the store after my first year in college. Instead, I got a job at the Spoor-Lasher Ready-Mix Concrete plant, just south of the Poughkeepsie Bridge. Dad had been friends with the owner, Mr. Spoor. I had ridden my bike to the plant, walked in the main office, introduced myself, and asked if they needed any help for the summer. The men smiled, and told me there was an opening on the loading dock. "Go talk to Ralph, down in the yard," I was told. As I departed, I heard the men chuckling, and one said, "I'll be surprised if he lasts twenty minutes!"

I found Ralph, a short, wiry Italian guy, who said he needed help loading cement onto the trucks. He took me upstairs into the warehouse, introduced me to Joe, a friendly Black guy in his mid-thirties, and then explained what the job entailed. He led me to a skid loaded with bags of cement; each one weighed a hundred pounds. Joe showed me how to tear off the necks of those bags of cement, then pour the contents into a chute that went into the trucks waiting below. Ralph would shout the number of bags needed for each batch, depending on the job. It sounded fun to me, and I readily agreed to do the job.

The first truck approached and Ralph shouted "Forty!" Joe grabbed the first bag, tore the neck off, and grabbed for the next one. I followed his lead. By the time that truck pulled away, the air was filled with concrete dust and my hands and shoulders were sore. Minutes later, the next truck pulled up, and after that one, another one. It was brutal work, and I was proud I kept up with Joe. By the end of the day, we must have handled five hundred bags apiece and my hands and body hurt like hell. When it was time to go home, Joe and Ralph shook my blistered, caked-with-cement-dust hand, and nodded their approval. While riding my bike up the hill from the river, I made up my mind to stick with it.

Joe had told me the only way to rid my hands of the cement goop was with Vaseline. I ignored his advice and tried washing them with soap and water, which made the paste even stickier. I finally used the Vaseline. I learned to follow his advice; he was, after all, at the top of the pecking order at the batching plant.

I returned the next day, and the day after that. I worked alongside Joe all summer, and despite the difference in our ages and cultures, we became pals. He was a short guy, but muscular and strong as hell. One day, I asked how much he thought he could carry. He replied, "Let's give it a go!" He grabbed one bag with his teeth, put one under each arm, and another on his back. Four hundred pounds! He then walked several feet. Most guys would collapse under that weight, but not Joe.

He was a different kind of mentor for me, a very thoughtful guy, who shared his world view with me when we weren't engaged in backbreaking labor. One afternoon, after I'd done something stupid, Joe said, "Franklin, I taught you everything I know and you still don't know nothing!" I never forgot that, especially since I tended to be a "know-it-all" kind of guy who could use a dose of humility. At the end of the summer, I returned to college, yet Joe continued loading cement trucks, I assume.

I never saw him again. Working at the cement plant made me realize how hard some people must work to make a living.

Follow Your Passion

When I returned to Syracuse in the fall, I rebelled again. Without consulting Mother, I switched my major from Business to Engineering. I enrolled in a course called "Advanced Laboratory" in the Physics department, even though my advisor told me it was only for students going on to graduate school. I pestered him so much, he suggested I call the professor, Dr. Charles Bachman, and discuss it. Dr. Bachman spoke with me at length on the phone, and then invited me to meet with him in his office. He consented to my taking the course as long as I read his book *Experimental Electronics*. The course would be based on it, he said.

His class was different, the most entertaining of any I'd taken at Syracuse. At any time during the semester, he said, I could take a verbal exam. If I passed with an A, I didn't have to attend class any more. Two weeks into the course, I told him I was ready for the final interrogation. He was surprised, but quizzed me for three hours. At the conclusion, he said, "You get an A, Frank. You don't have to come to class any more."

But I loved his class, I liked him, and I liked the other students. So I kept going. The work was fun: spectrophotometers, vacuum equipment, diffraction instruments, and induction heaters. From him I discovered that learning is fun if you have a great teacher.

Besides teaching, he collaborated with Dr. Robert O. Becker. They did extensive research on electronarcosis, and the electromagnetic effect on the central nervous system. Over time, he took on the role of surrogate father to me. He understood how my insatiably curious, and often obsessive, mind worked, and provided intellectual challenges, feedback and validation that I desperately needed. One day he produced a bushel basket of electronic parts:

brass flanges and tubing, faceplates, electron gun parts, meters, resistors, diffusion pumps, and high voltage transformers. "Frank," he said. "These are components of an electron diffraction system that we were building at GE. It was never properly assembled, and never worked. Do you want to give it a try?"

He had to know I couldn't wait to give it a go. A few sketches and a description of how it was supposed to work was all I needed. I sorted all the parts on a bench, roughed out what fitted and what was missing, and dove in. It took several weeks to assemble it—a vacuum system, high voltage power pack, electron gun and phosphor screen. I used a stainless steel mesh for the target and blew cigarette smoke on it to create a fine dust. We turned up the vacuum, rough and diffusion pumps, lit up the electron gun, cranked up the high voltage, and fired a highly-focused electron beam through the mesh. A beautiful circle, diffraction pattern appeared on the phosphor screen.

I raced down to Dr. Bachman's office, and saw, to my chagrin, that he was in a meeting. Patience has never been a strength of mine. I stood near the window in the hall and tapped on it. When I got his attention, I formed an "O" with the fingers of both hands. He smiled, excused himself from his meeting, and rushed to the lab with me. If we were kids, we'd be jumping up and down for joy. There's nothing like "inventor's high"—the thrill of creating something spectacular out of junk.

I can't imagine what my life would have been like if

I'd honored my mother's wishes to major in Business and manage Dad's jewelry store. You have to know what your passion is and go for it. Be true to yourself. My college years flew by because I did what I loved. But I didn't love college.

Although I was in the Honors Society, I was a terrible student; I felt certain I would have learned more on my own. In most classes I was a cocky, arrogant "know-it-all." I despised some of the department heads and had contempt for most of my teachers, many of whom were graduate students who knew less than me. I didn't challenge them; I was just indifferent. With the exception of Bachman's labs and my Friday morning class in Fluid Mechanics, I was bored silly. The worst was Steam and Power Plant Engineering, the only class I ever got a D in. I spent my free time drinking, dating, and discussing religion and politics with my frat brothers. Meeting Dr. Bachman and getting under his wing made college worth the trip.

Have Fun

I met lots of bright, fun guys in my college fraternity. Although we all had different college majors, and were serious about our studies, we shared a wicked sense of humor and enjoyed pranks. Our frat house was similar to the one in the movie "Animal House" with lots of drinking, hell raising and women. We didn't break laws, bully anyone, cheat on tests, or take advantage of others. But we had a helluva lot of fun.

"Once upon a midnight dreary while I pondered weak and weary," one of my fraternity brothers was studying medieval architecture. As part of a class project, he had to make a model of a medieval church. Making models was foreign to him, so he asked Rod Fibbs and me, fellow frat brothers, if we could help. I'd been building model airplanes for a long time. Rod and I presented him with a deal. We'd construct a guaranteed A plus medieval church out of cardboard and balsa wood, and then ceremoniously burn it after he'd gotten his grade.

The night of the burning, a group of frat brothers gathered in a room with a fireplace. Rod donned a black fraternity robe, perched raven-like on a big wooden desk, and recited Edgar Allen Poe's classic poem, "The Raven" in his best Vincent Price voice, as we squirted lighter fluid on the church, and lit it. As the smoke wafted upwards through the chimney, I wondered if we'd all go to hell. Well, I'm still inventing and building things, and Rod is a retired pediatrician in San Francisco. We both have yet to find out.

Shortly after I graduated from college, in 1952, my college sweetheart Florence Ratka and I were married. She was Catholic, and I wasn't, but the Poughkeepsie Catholic Church agreed to marry us, as long as, during the rehearsal, I didn't go up to the altar.

I had asked Henry Materosian, one of my frat brothers, to be my best man. Henry was of Armenian descent and had spent his childhood in Iran. At 22, he was quite "Americanized" and was howlingly funny. The nervous young priest assigned to marry us looked like he'd just graduated from seminary and we surmised this might be his first wedding. During the rehearsal, Henry, in one of his devilish moods, told the priest that he was a Muslim, and that he'd have to roll out his prayer rug in front of the altar, and pray to Allah, before he could partake in a Catholic church ceremony. Henry, of course, was just kidding, but told his story with a straight face. We all did our best to contain our laughter.

The young priest was taken aback, not sure how to respond to the best man. The next day, the priest seemed relieved that Henry didn't roll out his prayer rug during our wedding. I learned, several weeks later, that the priest left the clergy to pursue another profession. Apparently the priesthood was not his calling. I can't help wondering if we had something to do with that decision. In light of the current problems with Iran, I can't help wondering of Henry's fate as well.

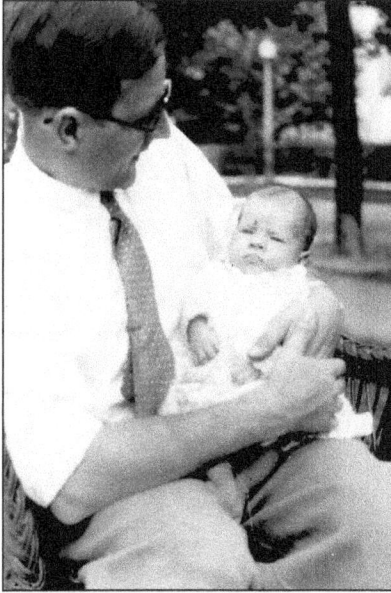

My father, Gerald Reick, with me in 1930

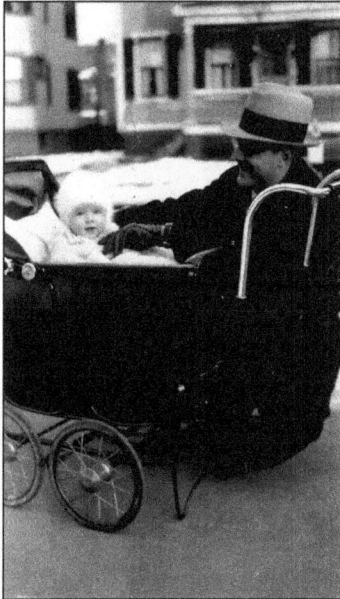

My dad and me at age 1

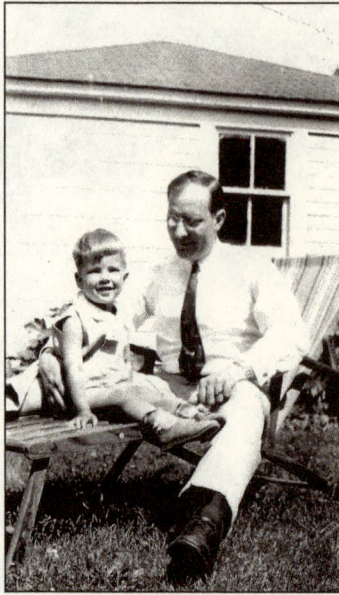

Dad and me, age 3, in backyard of Fox Terrace.

I was a 20th-century Huck Finn.
Taken at our camp near Red Oaks Mill.

The neighborhood kids at my 7th birthday party in Poughkeepsie. I am third from the right in the first row.

One of my first inventions. It was tippy.

Early entrepreneur

My parents, Bertha and Gerald Reick, with me near Red Oaks Mill

I played trumpet in the high school band, 1944.
As a freshman, I hadn't yet grown into the uniform.

POUGHKEEPSIE NEW YORKER

Poughkeepsie High Band to Give Spring Concert Friday Night

Poughkeepsie High school's band will present its annual spring concert Friday night at 8 o'clock in the school auditorium under the direction of Luther H. Hawkins. Franklin Reick is president of the band.

The first part of the program will be as follows: Brockelshire's "Glory of the Trumpets March," with majorettes Marilyn Rauh and Teresa Morrill; "The Fortune Teller Overture," Victor Herbert; "Chorale" from "Concert Suite" for four trombones, by Clapp, with Phillip Mylod, Alfred Kuenzelmann, Edward Bastian and Fred Wohlfahrt; Beethoven's "Adagio Cantabile," with horn solo by Joan Becker, accompanied by Dolores Riascher; "Safari Overture," G. E. Holmes.

The second section of the program will include "Straight Ahead March," A. R. Hodges, with majorettes Florence Nowik, Betty Robinson and Teresa Morrill; "The Student Prince Overture," Romberg; "Petite Melodie" (Clarinet quartet), Jane Kaman, Herbert Blaufarb, Bruce Griffing and Perry Seis; "Enchanteres," Vivien, saxophone solo by Nancy Waldron accompanied by Harold Vilaho, and "Elsa's Procession to the Cathedral," from "Lohengrin," Wagner.

The final section of the program will include a drill, "There's Something About a Soldier," with all majorettes participating and including Joanne Martin, Sylvia Whitman and Arline Hitchcock; "Light Cavalry Overture," Suppe; "Parade of the Wooden Soldiers," drum quartet with Albert Lutz, John Ducek, William Lewis and Larry Ong; "Believe Me If All Those Endearing Young Charms," with a trombone solo by John Binder accompanied by Joan Becker; "Music Maker March," with a twirling solo by Marie Welton; "The Cricket and the Bullfrog," clarinet, Cornelius Freer, saxophone, David Albert; and "Lights Out March."

FRANKLIN REICK, president of the Poughkeepsie High School band, which will present its annual spring concert Friday night in the school auditorium.

Newspaper article featuring me and my band concert, May 5, 1948

Me on a family fishing trip to Canada

High school friends Bud Ross and George Galucci with me (in center)

Family pet ducks Donald and Dopey enjoying backyard pool after rain

Last photo of my father, taken two months before he died in 1944.
My life changed dramatically after his death.

My diving helmet invention, shown with my friend John Vanderwater.

The Melody Kings, the high school dance band I organized.
That's me in the back row with the trumpet.

Rod Phibs with home-made diving apparatus
at Jamesville Reservoir in Syracuse.

Another view of Rod Phibs with home-made diving apparatus.

Wedding photo, 1951, with John Vanderwater, Florence's cousin Barbara, Florence, me, Bill Landis, and Henry Marterosian. The flower girl in the photo was her niece, Mary Ann.

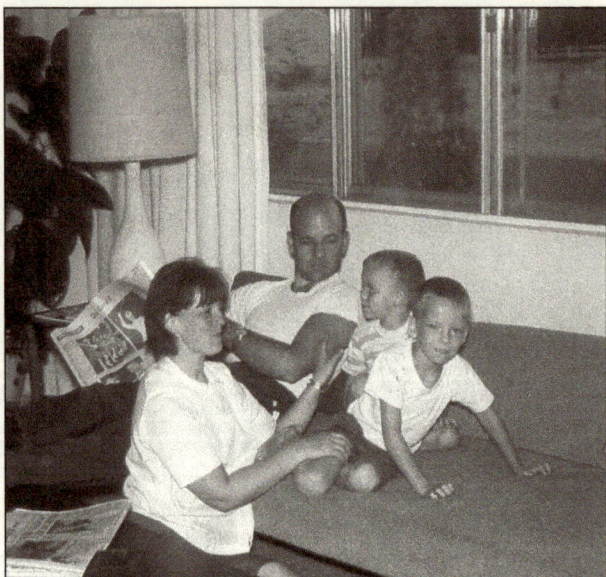

Florence, me, Kevin, and Gregg, with Steven on the way. I had just started my own business with Charles Bachman.

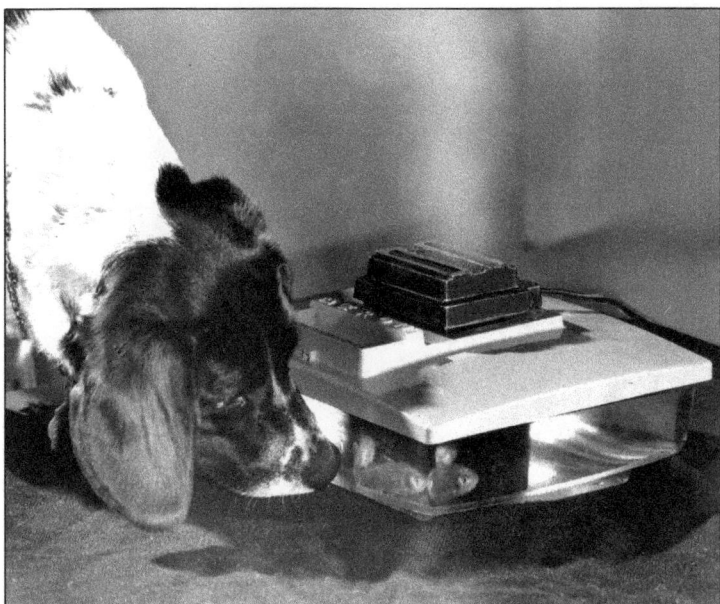

Public relations piece for steam vaporizer.
Goldfish swim in base; they fascinated our dog You You.

*The water never gets hot!

The remarkable Deluxe AERON vaporizer represents a new standard in steam vapor therapy. The AERON is designed and engineered for sickroom safety and convenience. There is no glass to shatter, no boiling over, and no scalding danger if water is accidentally spilled.

AUTOMATIC **AERON** VAPORIZER

ACCLAIMED BY PHYSICIANS AND PEDIATRICIANS

The vaporizer we invented that sold widely but briefly

The Oneida silver case that caused Worldcraft to go bankrupt

Caduceus carved by Richard Koontz

Burnco Smoker Accessories

A beautiful wood finish as reproduced in the handsome "Burnco Smoker Accessories" adds that important, distinctive touch to office or home furnishings. The wood finish accents and enhances any style of decor with its rich glow. These smoker accessories will be appreciated and kept by the recipient. Your goodwill is active throughout the years. Base is felt covered to protect desk or table top from scratches and marring. Available as individual pieces or as sets.

No. 4283-AT90, Ash Tray. *Size:* 5¾" x 5¾".

No. 4283-AT45, Ash Tray. *Size:* 3⅜" x 3⅜".

No. 4283-CB84, Cigarette Box. *Size:* 4¾" x 3½", inside.

No. 4283-CL70, Lighter.

No. 4283-AT90, 4283-AT45, 4283-CB84, 4283-CL70   1.05 — 2.7

Smoking set all designed and carved by Richard Koontz

*The family during ITT years in New Jersey:
me, Florence, Steven, Gregg, and Kevin*

The family at our home in Westwood, New Jersey,
after I left ITT and started Fluoramics

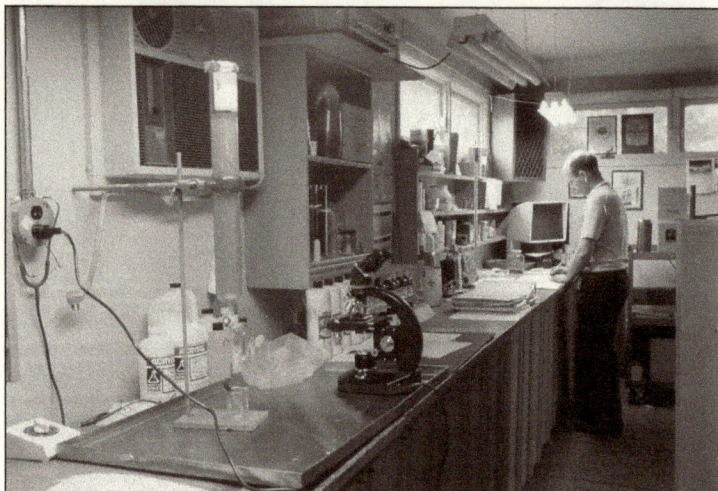

Early lab in my Westwood garage

Letter of commendation from Commander Mosier at Westover AFB, 1964

I was surrogate father to "Little Bug." We ran a series of animal stories as part of our Tufoil ad campaign. "Little Bug" was featured in one.

Sons Kevin and Gregg, early flying years at Ramapo Valley Airport.
I got my flying license when I was 41.

Writing in lab notebook (I have 42 total)

Testing Tufoil at my driveway in Westwood (Madman Frank's Garage)

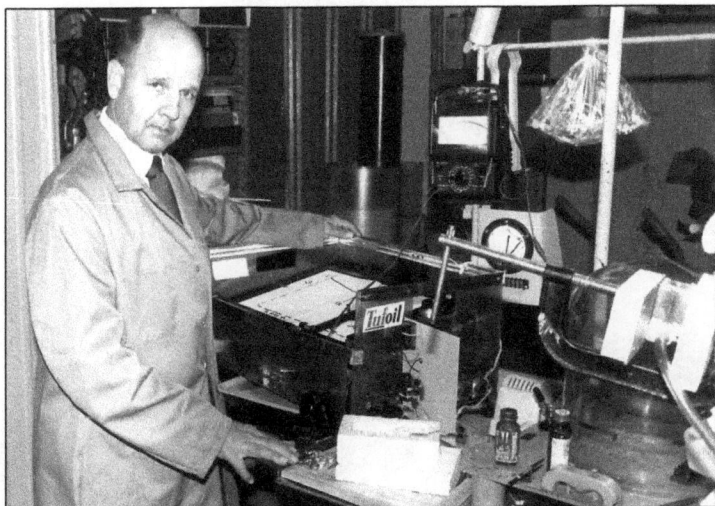

*Early superconductor work at our first plant
in Upper Saddle River, New Jersey*

George Castanis and I collaborated on SlikSilver toys,
which were sold internationally.

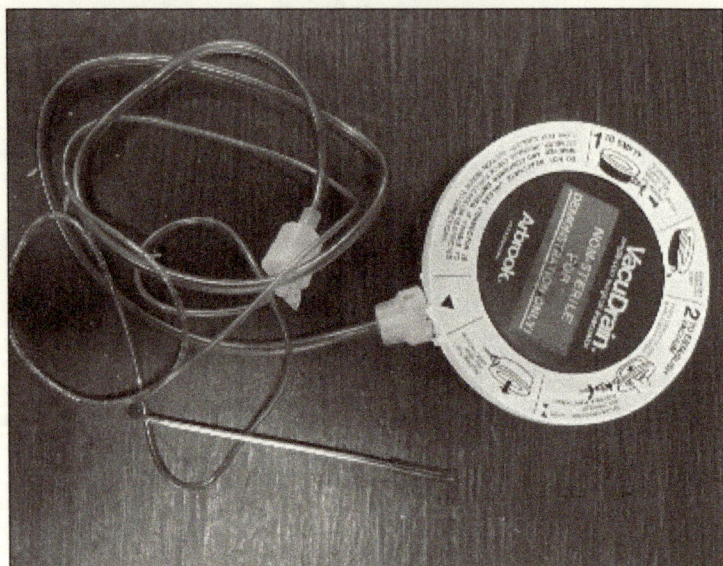

Surgical evacuator sold by Johnson and Johnson

Pouring liquid nitrogen for superconductor

Article in Popular Science *magazine*

*At the Chiang Memorial in Taiwan—with General Lu and me,
and Dr. Lee at far right, looking at the Chiang sarcophagus.*

Article in Design News that mentions Edison and me on the same page.

I received the New Jersey Inventor of the Year award in 1990.

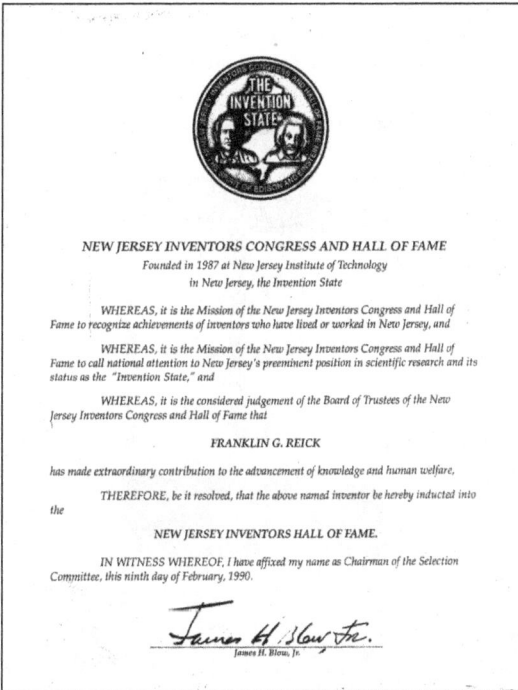

NEW JERSEY INVENTORS CONGRESS AND HALL OF FAME
Founded in 1987 at New Jersey Institute of Technology
in New Jersey, the Invention State

WHEREAS, it is the Mission of the New Jersey Inventors Congress and Hall of Fame to recognize achievements of inventors who have lived or worked in New Jersey, and

WHEREAS, it is the Mission of the New Jersey Inventors Congress and Hall of Fame to call national attention to New Jersey's preeminent position in scientific research and its status as the "Invention State," and

WHEREAS, it is the considered judgement of the Board of Trustees of the New Jersey Inventors Congress and Hall of Fame that

FRANKLIN G. REICK

has made extraordinary contribution to the advancement of knowledge and human welfare,

THEREFORE, be it resolved, that the above named inventor is hereby inducted into the

NEW JERSEY INVENTORS HALL OF FAME.

IN WITNESS WHEREOF, I have affixed my name as Chairman of the Selection Committee, this ninth day of February, 1990.

James H. Blow, Jr.

My Inventor's Hall of Fame Certificate

*Early Tufoil ad, done by office manager Paula Douglas and me.
They were very successful.*

Super-Hydrophobic sheet that lets gas through but not water

Photo of Dr. Charles Bachman at Jackson Hole, Wyoming, after he retired.

Ad for my first book, Flying the Stock Market *(Glenbridge Publishing, 1997), co-written with Bruce Siminoff*

CALDWELL
AIRPORT
CDW

Mr. Reich,

*Hope Santa brings you
all your favorite things.*

Merry Christmas

Thanks for being the
best pilot on the
Airport.

The Tower People

Caldwell Airport letter circa 1990

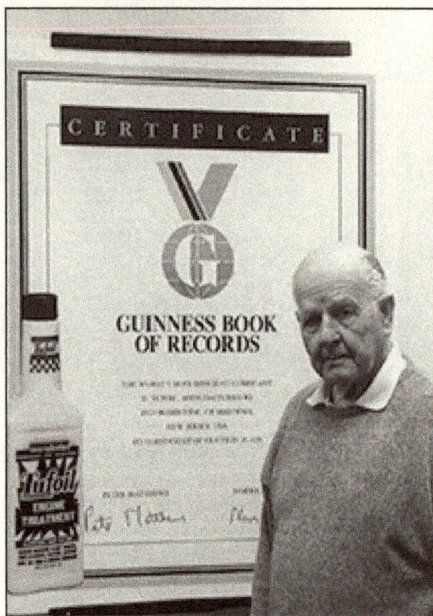

*Me in front of the Guinness Book of World Records certificate
for Tufoil, the world's most efficient lubricant.*

A page from my inventor's notebook from 1957

Me with my stack of notebooks

Office staff, circa 1992: Florence (holding Klutzie, the company mascot), Henri Nass, Phyllis Gloss, and Paula Douglas

With my plant manager Sederick Nelson, and Brandy

March 27, 1935, jewelry ad in the Poughkeepsie Eagle-News

Me at age 82 in 2013

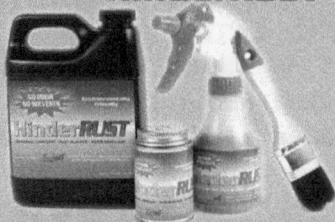

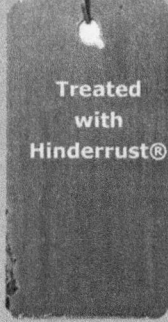
2013 Hinderrust Ad

PART
TWO

PART
TWO

Don't Divulge Your Secrets

I began my engineering career at General Electric at Electronics Park in Syracuse. It was the tail end of the vacuum tube era; they produced thousands of black and white 21" cathode ray tubes daily for televisions. Back then, televisions were huge as they had a large CRT and lots of vacuum tubes. The tubes would be transported throughout the plant on conveyor belts. It was all leading edge technology, quite a sight to behold.

Every so often, a group of Japanese engineers toured the plant. I was often asked to take them around the factory, to walk them through each process station, and answer any questions they had. Management never hinted they were potential competitors. The leader of the Japanese delegation, the one who asked the questions, always spoke perfect English. He would listen intently to the answer, then translate for the rest. I suspect they all understood English, for they all listened as I spoke, and nodded their heads when I made a technical point. After the tour, they spoke with great animation amongst themselves, always in Japanese. They also gave us elegant gifts at the end of the tour for sharing our intelligence.

It wasn't long before the Japanese developed CRTs cheaper and better than those we produced. Within a decade, CRTs were no longer produced in the U.S.; all emerging communications technology came out of Japan. The sharing of intelligence was a suicidal move on the part of GE. I continue to see examples of this today.

I recall lunchtime conversations with the electrical engineers who were working with newly developed discrete transistors. "These God-damned things aren't good for anything. All they do is blow out. They may be good for fuses, but that's it!" These were high impedance circuits that we used at the time: 90, 125 volts. Vacuum tubes work at those high voltages, but transistors work at low voltages. The transistors didn't fare well in the circuits the engineers were accustomed to. Years later, I remember similar nay-saying among the engineers when printed circuits first came out. They thought circuit boards were fantasies from another planet. Of course, now you can't find anything that's not printed circuits. The advances made due to miniaturization are incredible. My son Kevin works for IBM and they now have a chip with four billion, yes, *billion*, transistors on it!

Beware The Rat in a Tube

While still at GE, a labor strike shut down the vacuum tube plant. We engineers were sent to Buffalo where the company had another vacuum tube plant. There, we pretended to do useful work for several weeks, until the strike was resolved and we returned to Syracuse to start up the lines again.

Before startup, there are several checklists that have to be addressed—just like flying a plane—as there were an enormous number of tubes in process on the line when it was shut down. Some of the tubes were in the re-work area where they were re-processed and put back on the line. There was one tube in the system that we couldn't get to evacuate. It was very gassy. Everyone thought there must have been a leak in a tube or the apparatus. They went around with a leak detector and couldn't find anything. They kept pumping and pumping, to no avail. Finally, one of the engineers said, "Screw this!" and took the tube off the pump, cut the neck off, and found a dead rat in the tube.

Anyone who has worked around vacuum systems knows that a dead rat is going to take one hell of an effort to outgas (if ever). Although they don't smell as bad in a vacuum, because the organisms don't get to them, it's still one damn gassy thing to obstruct a vacuum tube. The term "dead rat in the system" has drifted into my lexicon since then. Every time I see something is plugged up, not smelling right, or not working properly, I say, "There's got to be a dead rat around someplace." I keep a stuffed rat in my office as a reminder.

As an Entrepreneur, Learn From the Big Lessons

In 1955, after four years working in the security of the corporate world, I left GE. I really didn't fit in well in a big institution. I was bored and disenchanted with the bureaucracy of the place. And I'm the kind of guy who needs to be a big fish in a small pond. I was an aloof, wet-behind-the ears smart-ass who believed if I couldn't run the place, I didn't want to be there.

Bachman and I formed a company called Diversified Technology, Inc. Our goal was to invent products that would make us millionaires. Several colleagues worked with us. I set up a laboratory in Bachman's basement, and stocked it with the many tools I'd acquired over the years—a drill press, lathe, and welding equipment. As I stepped into the unknown, along with my fellow novice entrepreneur/ inventors, my wife Florence took a steady job that helped pay the household bills for a few years until our first son was born. The five lessons below briefly summarize some of the more important lessons we all learned. The most important lesson is to learn from your mistakes and move on.

Our first venture at Diversified Technology was to create a better mold for beeswax candles after one of the partners noted that beeswax candles were difficult to mold because the wax stuck to everything. Beeswax candles were still made the old-fashioned way—repeated dipping. But they were the product of choice for the Catholic Church, so we thought we'd have a huge market. We invented molds that were saturated with water so the wax wouldn't stick to it. It took a year to develop the suitable materials, and the process worked well. The problem was that the local candle manufacturers didn't care about our new process. We'd gone through a year of work on speculation, and it was a big flop. The Big Lesson? *Meet Real Needs, Not Perceived Needs.*

Our next project was to develop a steam vaporizer that remained cool to touch. Bachman's idea was to use a wick to pull water up to a pair of electrodes where it was heated. It was more difficult than we expected, as electrodes and wicks were quickly destroyed in the process. Subsequently, I developed a process for making *in-situ* carbon electrodes in a glass fiber wick. I called them "graded boundary electrodes." The product life-tested well in the lab, and Bachman never complained about his electric bill, even though we had six to ten devices operating 24 hours a day.

Dean Minick, a former student of Richard Koontz, set up a company to manufacture and distribute our steam vaporizer. I moved the production machines to Mechanicsburg, Pennsylvania, where we built the product. He managed to get it distributed all over the U.S. Then disaster hit. We had done all our development work using water from Bachman's backyard well. The water in some areas had a high salt content. What resulted was the vaporizer would heat up, blow fuses, and in some cases, catch fire. Our product had failed. The Big Lesson? *Test Products Outside the Lab Before You Market Them.*

Another business partner, Harold Windsor, a chemist at GE, discovered that phenolics could be cast and molded in flexible molds to look just like wood. We formed a company called World Craft Inc., and made molds from the exquisite wood models that Koontz had made. We moved our operation into the vacant Kalfeltz Bakery Building in Syracuse, since the ovens and processing chemicals required more space. An added benefit was the low rent.

Our first big order was from Oneida Ltd, a silverware manufacturer, for silverware trays. We tooled up and went into production mode. I used an acid catalyst to trigger off the resin cure. It was not completely neutralized; it vaporized out of the plastic and discolored the silverware. Oneida cancelled the order due to poor quality of our product. We were broke, we had exhausted all our financial resources, and we declared bankruptcy. The Big Lesson? *Do Quality Control Before Mass Producing Your Product.*

You can't intellectualize failure. It feels like you're waist deep in shit in an outhouse and somebody's pissing on you. I was only 32, and had a wife and two pre-school kids, with one on the way. I had no income, and no prospects. My mind raced, I couldn't sleep at night, and I spent my days in cold sweat-producing fear. I was at the lowest point of my existence, and I went through the process of mentally dying, similar to what a drug addict must go through before finally entering rehab and becoming "reborn."

When things were at their lowest, I was saved by a phone call from Chuck Aldrich, one of my fraternity brothers. He was working on a top-secret government program at ITT in New Jersey. They had a lot of bright engineers on their staff, he told me, but none of them were handy.

"Do you want a job?" he asked. *Did I want a job?* His timing was exquisite. As much as I enjoyed being an inventor and entrepreneur, albeit a bankrupt one, I had to support my family. And from what Chuck said, I'd still be doing what I loved—making things work. The Big Lesson? *Learn to Deal With Failure.*

A week later, I packed my lathe, drill press, and tools in a U-Haul trailer, and hooked it to the back of our car. It was top heavy, but in my eagerness to start a new job, I wasn't concerned. I packed Florence and the boys, as well as the family dog, into the car, and we began the five-hour drive to Poughkeepsie, New York, where they'd stay with her parents until I found us a house in New Jersey.

Shortly after we got to cruising speed on the freeway, the trailer started to oscillate. It swerved from side to side slightly, then began thrashing like the inner tub of an overfilled washing machine during the spin cycle. It was a nightmare that seemed to go on for an eternity! I couldn't brake for fear of flipping over. The car finally slowed down enough that I could pull over to the side of the road.

My legs were rubbery and I was drenched in sweat. It was as close to a near death experience I'd ever had. A trucker had witnessed it, and pulled up behind us. "You're lucky to be alive," he told me, out of the earshot of my wife. "I thought you were going to flip over." After I regained my composure, I continued driving, but at a much reduced speed. I'm a daredevil by nature, but I wasn't taking any chances with my family. This wasn't a lesson I learned as an entrepreneur, but just a lesson in life. Maybe the most important one. Family first. I am grateful to this day for the deity that took grace on us. The Big Lesson? *Don't Lose Sight of What's Most Important in Your Life.*

Be A Hero, Even When Nobody Knows About It

I spent a total of six years working at ITT, during the height of the Cold War with the Soviet Union. ITT was a huge military-industrial corporation, bigger than AT&T. The Cuban Missile Crisis had taken place in October 1962, when President Kennedy and Soviet Premier Nikita Krushchev went eyeball to eyeball. That led to an American naval embargo at Cuba, the Bay of Pigs, one that could have started World War III. A year later, in November 1963, President Kennedy was assassinated in Dallas. Tensions ran high. Was an attack coming from our Soviet adversaries? Were Cuba and/or the Soviet Union behind the Kennedy assassination? Our military was on high alert.

Initially I worked at the ITT Data and Information Systems Division (DISD) in Paramus, New Jersey. We worked on the Strategic Air Command (SACC) display generators that would alert us if the Soviets launched a nuclear first strike against the U.S. The U.S. had four interconnected command centers that comprised the command and control system for SACC scattered around the country.

A display generator displayed maps, photos, radar images, and electronic messages onto large display screens that generals and decision makers could review—similar to the command center depicted in the movie *Dr. Strangelove*. By today's standards the electronics were primitive, but back then, they were state of the art. It was the early age of computer technology. IBM was making punch cards and the computer as we know it didn't exist. It was the beginning of the solid state era, before Microsoft and Apple had been formed. The Xerox copy machine had just been invented and FAX technology was years away.

One day I was called into my manager's office. "Frank, we've got a big problem. The display generators at the command centers aren't working. For all practical purposes, the system is out of action. What do you think you can do about it?"

ITT had designed those display systems, and at a crucial time, they stopped operating. The Soviets could launch a first strike and we'd not know it!

I told my manager I had to see what the problem was

before I could say, with any accuracy, if I could fix it. He told me I'd have to go to the command center inside a mountain near Westover Air Force Base in Massachusetts. It was a top secret location, and required the highest security clearance.

I already had Top Secret clearance; it was required in order to work for ITT's Military Systems Unit. When I applied for the job, I had to outline everything I'd done from my birth to the day I filled out the form. Then the FBI investigated me, and called friends and acquaintances. A few of them called me to say, in jest, "Frank, I knew they were going to get you sooner or later." When I finally got the clearance, I felt like I'd made the big leagues. I'd get to work on top secret projects with really bright and congenial men. I knew I hadn't been hired for my intelligence, but my skills with machines. My big day had come.

"They'll be waiting for you," I was told. I drove up to Westover Mountain in a rented car with the maps and the necessary paperwork they provided. I arrived in the early morning, parked the car, and approached two steel blast doors that were wide open. Two soldiers stood guard at a desk. Television monitors tracked my every move. As I approached the desk, one of the soldiers said, "Hello, Mr. Reick. We've been expecting you." I noticed a photograph of me, attached to more paperwork, on his desk. It was like a scene from a James Bond movie.

I was cleared to go to a second desk, inside the

mountain, where I was once again greeted, and assigned to a sergeant, who never left my side. *Ever.* I soon realized that in a top secret military facility, you leave your privacy behind at the front door. He led me to the office of the officer in charge of the facility, which more resembled the interior of a modern, elaborate corporate headquarters than the inside of a mountain. The Major briefed me on the problem, then showed me the display generator area. It was a beehive of activity—soldiers sitting at consoles, headsets on, twiddling dials. It took several hours to show me how the equipment was supposed to work.

After I'd checked into the local motel, I was alone, and had some time to think. (I was only accompanied by the sergeant *within* the facility). The next morning, I told the Major I could fix the problem, but only in my machine shop in my basement. That posed a major security problem. The Major thought about it, then said, "Frank, let me have the keys to your car." An hour later, he returned my keys and said, "Frank, don't open the trunk until you get home."

I drove back to New Jersey with the top-secret display pump system in my trunk. After taking it to my basement, I met with several managers at work, told them what the problem was, and said, "I can fix this, but I need some help." I suggested the names of some gifted engineers I'd worked with. They discussed my request and replied, "Okay Frank, it's yours. Here's the charge number for materials."

My colleagues and I began work on my kitchen table. First we dissected the apparatus and spent several days discussing our strategy. We then purchased the materials needed and commenced the work in my basement. In less than a week, we had a working prototype. We showed it to management, generated the necessary paperwork, and I drove back to Westover with the fixed generator in my trunk.

Once again, I walked through the blast door and was greeted in the same way by the guard. I continued on, past the right-angle bend, where my sergeant awaited me. He ushered me into the Major's office, and I handed over the car keys. The Major left the room for a few moments, then returned to hear my explanation of what we'd done. An hour later, he led me to the display generator, where everything was hooked up and running. He seemed greatly relieved.

That night, he invited me to the Officer's Club with his fellow brass, and we drank a few more than I was used to. I drove home the next day, slightly hungover but happy. I arrived back at work to find I was "the talk of ITT." We had fixed a piece of equipment that was integral to our national defense at the time when global tensions between the Soviet Union and the U.S. were at an all-time high. I was proud to have done my part to keep our complex early warning system functioning. For two weeks at ITT, I was a hero and walked on water. About a year later, that division shut down, in a political move I never understood.

Make and Follow Practical Rules

Since that experience and numerous others, I've put together my own list of what to do when things don't go as expected. Murphy did a grand job with his laws showing what can go wrong in the world of technology but he didn't expend much energy showing how to get out of trouble once you're in it. Hence, I developed Reick's Rules for Troubleshooting. . . .

1. *What was the last thing you did?*

2. *It ain't ever what you think it is! (The solution to the problem, that is.)*

3. *Whenever you're absolutely sure of what the problem is, you're wrong! (A conclusion jumped to is always wrong!)*

4. *If you can't find the trouble, wiggle everything in sight. Sparks and static are strong indicators! Unplug it and plug it in again.*

5. *Machines tend to lurk, plotting outages years down the line. Example: dry solder joints wait for a long time before a trace of corrosion puts them out of service.*

6. *Remember the alpha male in a wolf pack. If you approach the machine cowering with your tail between your legs, you don't have a chance!*

7. *Never swear or have a temper tantrum near a machine. They can sense your frustration and will only make things worse!*

8. *Don't try to be clever. The simplest solution is usually the correct one. Complicated solutions are always wrong.*

9. *Nothing is easy.*

10. *Finally...Never let a machine win. It helps if you are obsessive compulsive.*

Accept Compliments

After two years in Paramus, I survived a corporate-wide layoff and was transferred to the research labs in Nutley, New Jersey. There I was assigned to several interesting projects during the Cold War. The big buzzwords of the day were measure and countermeasure. We did something, they did something better; we'd go back to the drawing board, and on and on, all in the pursuit of the best tools for mutual destruction. Competition makes for great technological advances. Too bad it wasn't for a good cause.

I worked with Dr. Lucio Velesi, a brilliant but temperamental scientist, on the development of a broadband device that could detect radar signals sent by the Russians, no matter the frequency. The project was based on work done by Dr. Arditi, many years earlier, with resonances in rubidium vapor. If you put those resonant frequencies in a magnetic field, you could run the resonant point up to higher and higher frequencies. The idea was to run detection up and down the Xband and use it as a detector for different frequencies. It was a clever idea.

I was brought in only after two other engineers had thrown up their hands. They assigned a technician named Doug Scharp to work with me. We got along great from the start, and over the next few months, as we worked with big magnets and discovered a way to detect resonant signals as we changed the magnetic field, I came to realize he was one of the brightest, and most down to earth, men I'd ever met. We were on an inventor's high throughout the duration of the project. Once we'd achieved our objectives, I trained Dr. Velesi and he demonstrated it to the contractor at ROME Air Development Center. They paid for it, and that was the end of the project. It was never used because it required such heavy magnets, and was impractical. At the time, we didn't have cobalt samarium, which weighed much less.

By far, one of the most meaningful compliments I've ever received, although it wasn't meant for my ears, was a conversation I overheard in the break room. Doug was telling other techs, "Put Reick on a desert island and in six months he'd be living like a king." I never forgot that. In the world of an inventor, the thrill is the realization that your invention works as intended. Accolades are nice, but mean far more when coming from a peer.

Take Second Chances

After the excitement of working on the Xband detector and the thrill of walking on water after fixing the display generator wore off, I was becoming more and more disillusioned with the culture of ITT. It may have had an opulent facade, but it was no longer a vibrant, healthy company. Like General Electric, ITT had become bloated with bureaucracy; instead of growth, it was in a period of decay. Instead of making proactive decisions, managers were always reacting, which wasn't to my liking.

Many of my creative co-workers who survived lay-offs became as disgusted as me with the corporate politics, but stayed on for the job security and benefits. I was making $24,000 a year, which was lots of money then, but I was never motivated by the money. I needed meaningful and challenging work.

While still working at ITT, I realized nobody had a good system for sealing oxygen services for welding and steel making. Oxygen is a tricky material and if not handled correctly, can cause explosions. In my spare time, I developed a pipe dope (thread sealant) product that could be used in gaseous and liquid oxygen applications. We called it Formula 8. It required no curing time, and could be used in hard-to-reach applications. We made the product in my garage, packaged it by hand in aluminum tubes, and taped on labels. We sent out press releases to all the industrial magazines, tabloids and journals, and much to my amazement, we started getting orders. My primary customer was the Lindy Corporation, which produced bottled gases. Dave Noland did the testing for us.

I was having fun doing my own thing out of my garage. For years I'd wanted to be my own boss; I realized now was the time. At 42, I had a product that showed promise, and I said to myself, "I will either succeed on my own or die!" So I quit ITT. I chose Fluoramics as my company's name, a composite derived from "fluoro-carbon" and "dynamics."

I can't say that my wife was thrilled that I quit my

job. She was home with three rambunctious boys, all budding inventors, and she worried enough for both of us. I've never been a worrier, and never saw a problem solved by worry. But Florence was very supportive and handled the financial part of the fledgling business.

Sales of Formula 8 grew by leaps and bounds, and we moved production out of my garage to a bigger building. By that time I was flying a Beechcraft V-tail Bonanza. Life as an inventor/entrepreneur was good. We moved to an office in Upper Saddle River. We later occupied our current 26,000 square foot factory in Mahwah.

Timing is Everything

The word got around that, if you needed a better lubricant, call Frank. One day I got a phone call from Charlie Nestor, the chief training officer at FLETC, the Federal Law Enforcement Training Center, in Brunswick, Georgia.

"I need a better gun lubricant, Frank," he said. I told him I'd see what I could do. I went into my lab and a few weeks later, sent some samples to him.

Charlie called me back and said, "That was pretty good, Frank, but..." That meant I had to go back to the lab. It's a big operation down there, next to a decent-sized airport. It was an excuse to fly my plane down there to meet with him. Each time, I brought a new and improved product. He always ended our meeting with a "but." His final "but" was a request for more rust inhibitor.

"You gotta be crazy!" I told him. "I know you can do

it, Frank," he replied, and used the golden word "standardize." I did it, and they began using our new GunCoat lubricant.

On one of my trips down there, Charlie said, "Frank, we've got a new shooting simulator I want you to see." He took me into a room that held a color television projection system, a seat resembling the front seat of a car, and a screen with dangling strips on it. The simulator projected an image on the screen, and the person in the chair was supposed to interact with the image.

Charlie gave me a pistol with blanks, told me to watch the screen, and shoot when appropriate. The simulation tested your reflexes. "After you pull the trigger," he said, "all action will freeze and we can see how good a marksman you are." The simulation had me riding down the highway in the passenger seat of a police car. A speeder passed us on the left. My "partner" turned on the red lights and siren and made him pull over.

A raunchy guy with a beard and filthy tee shirt approached our car, saying, "Whaddaya bothering me for? I ain't doin' nothin'."

My partner and I both exited the car. My partner asked, "What's in the trunk?"

"Nuthin', man," the guy replied. "Leave me alone!" He then opened the trunk, saying, "You wanna know what's in the trunk?" and pulled out a pistol and shot my partner! I aimed my gun and POW! I shot him, right in the chest. The screen froze. Charlie and I walked up to the screen and saw the bullet mark. I'd never shot a pistol in my life, and was feeling proud of myself for "killing" the bad guy.

Instead of praise, Charlie said, "You flunked, Frank. Your partner's dead. You were a few seconds late." So that was my education on firing a gun. Timing is everything.

Don't Wait for Others to Toot Your Horn!

During the mid-1980s, every inventor with a bathtub and canoe paddle mixed Teflon powder in oil and made outrageous claims about what it would do for an engine. The term "mouse milk" was the derogatory term, in technical circles, which described these lubricant products. The American public fell for the advertising scams and bought millions of dollars of this stuff.

During the height of the "mouse milk" era, I was awarded several patents on Tufoil (pronounced TUFF-oil), a lubricant I invented that has a very low surface friction. The idea for Tufoil came one day when I was flying down the corridor in New York City. I saw the crud coming up from the canyons and I figured I'd have to do something about all that automobile exhaust.

I spent eight years working on Tufoil. At one time, during the testing phase, my driveway looked like Madman Frank's Used Car Lot. My sons and I were pulling engines and doing round the clock experimental work. I had a Ford Thunderbird "T-Bird" with a huge 460 engine. We used to be in and out of that crankcase on a weekly basis. I got so good at pulling that engine apart, I didn't even bother to put the chassis crossbars in—we sawed them out underneath the crankcase so we could get it out easier. We only used four bolts to put the pan back so we could remove it in a hurry. I could pull a set of rod and main bearings in a couple of hours and put new ones in.

During those years of development, I had several formulations that were hard on copper, so it was imperative that I got in and out and replaced those bearings. No power on earth could get me to do that again. The last place in the world I want to be is lying underneath a car with oil dripping on my face while replacing rod and main bearings. That was another rite of passage for me, I guess, one I had to go through.

When Tufoil was introduced into the marketplace, it was initially sold at Pep Boys, True Value Hardware stores, Kmart and other retailers. I knew Tufoil was good, but didn't know *how good* until one of our distributors contacted me and said information had leaked out that the National Bureau of Standards (NBS) had tested it with spectacular results. The testing, I learned, had been done by Dr. Stephen Hsu. I had met him a few years earlier, at a meeting of the American Society of Lubricant Engineers (ASLE). At that time I had made several inquiries about NBS's tests on my product, but had gotten no response. I finally requested the information through the Freedom of Information Act through my Washington attorney John White and Senator Bradley.

To my surprise, Dr. Hsu called me at home one evening. "Frank," he said, "Let's get together and go over this." I flew my Bonanza to Gaithersburg, MD airport on December 11, 1986. I then took a cab to his office at NBS. His first words to me were, "Frank, I would have sold my soul to have done what you did."

I spoke with Dr. Hsu for two-and-a-half hours, mostly about the technology. After I left, I never heard from him again. I did, however, hear from their attorneys that I couldn't mention the results of their tests in our advertising, as they were congressionally mandated not to endorse products. My secretary Paula took the report and corresponded with the Guinness Book of World Records. A year later, Tufoil made the Guinness Book of Records, listed as the World's Most Efficient Lubricant with a coefficient of friction of .029. The question I always ask myself is, "Why did the NBS try to suppress this information and what else have they suppressed over the years?"

We got the word out ourselves, and Tufoil is now our flagship product that is used widely across the globe in industrial and consumer applications. It's a popular general lubricant used in gearboxes and engines to reduce friction, wear, noise, and operating temperature, and to preserve and extend the lifespan of machinery.

In Business, Profit is the Bottom Line

We did our own public relations and advertising for Tufoil, but with that type of product, you need distributors to do your marketing and selling. The ideal distributors for Tufoil were large auto retail chains. I met with the Sales Manager of one of them, on the West Coast, who seemed gung-ho on our product. "This is going to be a f—hot seller, Frank!" he told me. "Ship us all you got!"

I told him it would take millions of dollars to advertise our product and we had limited resources. He looked me in the eye and said, "Frank, you put shit in ice cream buckets and advertise it, and we will sell your product."

We shipped a truckload of product to their stores. We gave them favorable payment terms, an advertising allowance, and hoped for success. But I was taken aback by his constant crude and undignified talk.

Before the year was out, I found out his operation was just as crude. They disregarded our payment terms and took advertising allowances that weren't properly documented. The final outrage was a bill we got at the end of the year for inventory shrinkage. *Inventory shrinkage?* They claimed we were liable for products stolen off their shelves! My accountant tallied it all up and found we hadn't made any money on that "big deal" at all.

"Frank," he said, "that was a big waste of time." High volume and zero profits are ridiculous. We decided to seek different channels of distribution.

Know When to Delegate

Despite that shady distributor, Tufoil was doing phenomenally well, and it was time to investigate the international market. In October 1979, I spent a week in Taiwan visiting potential distributors. I went with our

West Coast sales rep. It was the first time I'd spent seventeen hours in an airplane. A subtle form of gangrene in the lower spine develops after a trip like that. Between the jet lag and the lack of circulation, I don't know how international business people make that commute on a regular basis.

Taipei, the capital, was a gorgeous place—lush and green. The people were friendly, courteous and cheerful. I was treated like a head of state on my all-expenses-paid visit. We were met at the airport by the president of the Chinese Federation of Labor, treated to lavish meals, taken by limo to places of culture and to oil refineries. My first dinner was hosted by Shu Nai, a past Minister of Economics. I was also the guest of honor at a luncheon hosted by the chairman of the Petrochemical Industries Association of Taiwan. I even had a visit with the country's Vice President. I felt they'd mixed me up with Dr. Henry Kissinger!

I gave two dozen lectures on Tufoil, to over 300 Chinese scientists and engineers, during my week there. All the lectures were simultaneously translated by Dr. Laurence Lee. And after every lecture, I was treated to a lavish Chinese meal, often eating mystery food. The good news was that everyone seemed excited about Tufoil. The bad news was that I ate something that didn't agree with me on my last day there, and spent much of the trip back in the plane's lavatory.

When my sales rep and I got back to the West Coast, I dictated six tapes with details and recollections of the trip while it was fresh in my mind. By the time I reached New Jersey, between the food poisoning and the twelve-hour jet lag, I was exhausted. I turned the project over to my sales manager, which I later learned was a major cultural mistake. The Chinese were deeply offended that I didn't handle the deal personally. As a result, the whole deal unraveled at the seams. One thing I take pride in is that I'm a good delegator. But you have to know when to delegate and when to take charge.

Find A Great Patent Attorney

Every inventor, no matter how successful, needs a patent attorney. Mike Ebert was mine. He was a gracious and funny man universally admired by his clients, and one of the smartest men I've ever known. I met him in 1974 after I left ITT and had started my own company. From the get-go, we clicked intellectually. Mike helped me obtain dozens of patents, and we became lifelong friends.

Mike's first career was as an engineer, a requirement to be a patent attorney. As a patent attorney, he facilitated 903 patents, including coffeemakers, TV dinners, ultrasonic oxygenation instruments, and my Tufoil lubricant. He often referred to his clients as "the best and the brightest" on the planet, but *his* light shone the brightest. One of his first clients was Chester Carlson, a research engineer who had developed the xerographic process in 1938. It took Carlson eight years to find an investor in his new technology. He was turned down by IBM and the U.S. Army Signal Corps before the Haloid

Corporation, later the Xerox Corporation, "saw the light."

Mike was Carlson's patent attorney and was later offered a job as Xerox's chief patent counsel. He turned down the job because he didn't see a future in that business! He often joked that he had a genius for missing the boat on great opportunities. He later joined a patent firm in Manhattan and represented a number of famous personalities, including Salvador Dali.

Every year, Mike hosted an annual client party at his home in Mamaroneck, New York. He introduced me to many of them, many of whom became my lifelong friends. They were a fraternity of witty, bright creatives, who, in lively and humorous conversations, shared their recent success stories, and colossal failures, as inventors. They had large personalities, cursed a lot, and didn't care what others thought of them.

I met so many kindred spirits at those gatherings, many of whom inspire and challenge me to this day. It wasn't unusual to hear that an inventor who had made millions one year went bankrupt the next. There was, after all, a fine line between success and failure for inventors. But when we gathered at Mike's, nobody was whining or gloating. Inventors are eternal optimists who find daily joy in inventing and being creative, not basking in their success or drowning in their sorrows. Needless to say, for years, we all looked forward to gathering at Mike's "inventors' salon."

Mike was both a prolific writer and a voracious

reader. He corresponded with each of his inventors, often including inspirational quotes from great philosophers and historic world leaders, in his letters. I alone have a file of his letters that's two-and-a-half feet thick! His letters reflect his wit, knowledge of world affairs, and intelligence. They're filled with musings on religion, politics, the environment, and the arts. In both letters and conversations, he shared relevant quotes from Aristotle to Shakespeare. He was a genius at putting on white gloves, taking a rapier, and skewering his opposition. Here's an example of a letter he sent me on November 3, 1989:

> *Dear Frank,*
>
> *Whenever you shout "I won't let that Machiavellian bastard get away with it!" and I see smoke spouting from your ears, I assume you are pissed off at somebody. (I'm a sharp observer.) But I must insist that hereafter you not take the name of Machiavelli in vain.*
>
> *Long before Karl Marx, Niccolo Machiavelli recognized that in any society, the rules of the game favored those in power. He was not the enemy of decency and betterment. What the great Machiavelli taught is that if you aim to make changes for the better, you cannot change the rules of the game, but must manipulate these rules to your own advantage.*
>
> *Thus, in addressing the innovator, Machiavelli in Il Principe: 1413, said,*

—There is nothing more difficult to take in hand, more perilous to conduct or more uncertain in its success than to take the lead in the introduction of a new order of things, because the innovator has for enemies all those who have done well under the old conditions, and lukewarm defenders in those who may do well under the new.—

Sincerely,
Mike

Mike gave lectures at Cooper Union on patent law. He often brought me along as his "show and tell" inventor. He once joked, "Frank, I'm smarter than you and I write a helluva lot better than you. How come you can invent things and I can't?" I've often thought about that and have come to the conclusion that all great inventors have an edginess, a streak of insanity in them. Their "insanity" manifests in different ways: strange eating habits, temper tantrums, obsessive behavior. (The biography of Steve Jobs is a good example of this.) Mike didn't have that. He was just a regular guy, a brilliant regular guy. As I watch the intellectual mediocrities in our government, I consider myself blessed to have associated with this truly great man, who was like a big brother to me.

Fraternize With Other Inventors

One of the 'large personalities" I met at Mike's parties was Dr. Joe Wilder, the Chief of Surgery at the Hospital for Joint Diseases at NYU and a professor of surgery at Mount Sinai Hospital. Although a surgeon by trade, Joe was an idea man, but lacked what it takes to realize those ideas. Even though I knew nothing about the world of surgery, Joe often invited me to visit him at the hospital. He'd give me a white coat and a mask and usher me, God-like, into the operating rooms, where operations with names like *oopherectomy* and *cholycystectomy* were in progress.

"Take a look," he'd insist, and I'd peer into the viscera. The surgeons were all polite, and willing to talk to me about what they were doing as they used various tools to slice, retract, extract, and suture tissue back into place. I found the art of surgery, and all the tools that accompanied it, fascinating. It was what I did as a little kid with my own tools. I took things apart and put them back together, except the surgeons were doing it on people.

One day, while Joe and I were conversing around a long conference table in his office, he threw a surgical evacuator across the table toward me. He exclaimed, "Goddamn it, Frank! We use a lot of these around here. There ought to be some way we could invent a better product to compete with it." I took it home to examine it. It was basically a compressed bellows attached to a tube filled with small holes. The tube was inserted into the wound. As the bellows expanded, it created a vacuum that drained blood and serum from the wound for a few days.

I sat the thing on my desk and had no idea how I'd

improve on it. Then a light bulb went off in my head. I'd reverse-engineer the thing! Within eight hours I had vacuum formed a cup, put a rubber membrane across the top, a tube on the side, and pushed the membrane down to create a vacuum. The original had a flexible wall; mine had a stiff wall. The original had a stiff bottom; mine had a flexible bottom. When Joe and I tried it out on a patient, it not only worked, but it worked better!

Wilder called the president of Johnson and Johnson to tell him about our new and improved closed-wound suction system. Within two weeks, we licensed it, and it was sold worldwide, as VacuDrain, for a couple of years. J & J made a mistake on the choice of rubber for the membrane. It didn't age well, and some other aspiring inventor improved on it. But I was proud of it.

Wilder was once called in to provide a surgical opinion on a celebrity who'd been hit by a bus in Manhattan. The celebrity's leg was crushed and two other surgeons had insisted they'd have to amputate. Wilder strode in, examined the leg, and said, "I can save this leg." And he did. The recuperation took several months, and the two became friends. The patient was an artist, musician and actor. When Wilder told him he longed to do something with art, the patient suggested he take up painting. And he did.

His first paintings were crude, but he had a good sense of color and learned quickly. Joe became passionate about his paintings, and within a few years, several were selected to hang in galleries. Joe died in 2003 from a heart attack. The headline in his *New York Times* obituary was *Joseph Wilder, 82, Surgeon and Skilled Artist.*

Collaborate with Other Inventors

Another inventor I befriended as a result of my association with Mike was George Castanis, a successful toy designer. Through him I met dozens of people in the toy industry, all interesting characters! The toy world is a story in itself. In the seventies, George and I collaborated on the SlikSilver toys which we licensed to Mego Corporation. They were hand-held manipulation games with superhydrophobic surfaces. They resembled miniature pinball machines, but instead of metal balls, they were mercury-like water balls. These "incredible water-action games," as the TV ads portrayed them, had names like "DamBuster," "Canyon" and "Citadel." The games sold well until games like Nintendo became the new rage. Both the SlikSilver toys and Nintendo are considered vintage toys today.

Be Inspired By Other Inventors

One of the most prolific inventors I met through Mike Ebert was Maurice Kanbar. Besides holding over thirty patents for things such as lint removers, hypodermic needle protectors, and a cryogenic cataract remover, Maurice is a philanthropist, real-estate magnate, film producer (*Hoodwinked*), author (*Secrets from an Inventor's Notebook*), and the founder of Quad Cinemas, New York's first multiplex cinema. NYU's Tisch School for the Arts named its Institute for Film and Television after him. One of the reasons Maurice is a wealthy man is because he knows how to market his inventions. We became close friends and collaborated on a couple of projects. He also became a surrogate uncle to my sons.

One day he said to me, "Frank, I want to make a better vodka, one that doesn't give me a headache after I drink it." I replied, "The world doesn't need a better vodka, Maurice." There were so many other things to invent.

But Maurice was a man possessed when an intriguing idea came to him. As with most inventions, the inspiration, combined with serendipity, led to the "invention" of SKYY vodka, famous for its blue bottle. Maurice recalled how he came up with the name for his vodka. He had bought a twelve-story building in Pacific Heights that overlooked the San Francisco Bay and Alcatraz. Looking out the window one day, the normally overcast sky was a brilliant sky blue. Not a cloud in sight! Blue sky! Blue bottle! Eureka!

He sold millions of blue bottles of SKYY vodka in the two years he ran the business. But he was an inventor at heart, and grew weary running a company. He sold the company to Campari. Since then, he "invented" the vodka-based Vermeer Dutch Chocolate Cream liqueur and Blue Angel Premium Vodka.

On one trip to visit Maurice in San Francisco, a group of us went out for Chinese food. The group included his friend Michael Savage and his family. Michael is a biologist, author and host of the nationally syndicated radio show, The Savage Nation. He's written a number of *New York Times* bestsellers on topics ranging from politics to herbal medicine and homeopathy. He's known for his rants, and, as you can well imagine, our conversation was lively. During dinner, I brought up my own Theory on Evolution. My daughter-in-law, Geri McCall Reick, had just published an exquisitely illustrated book on dinosaurs, and she and I had had many discussions on this subject while she did her research.

I told them that I believed that intelligence is an evolutionary dead end, just another of nature's experiments that had no long-term value. All the highly evolved creatures that preceded us for millions of years have vanished as the world changed.

To illustrate my theory, I used the distance from San Francisco, where we were dining, to my home in Westwood, New Jersey to paint a timeline: 2568 miles or 162,700,000 inches. If each inch represented a million years, then a mere sixty-five inches represented the age of Tyrannosaurs Rex. If one inch is 100,000 years, then one hundredth of an inch takes us back to the end of the last Ice Age, when this global warming epic began. One millionth of an inch is a hundred years, when modern technology and the airplane were invented—about the thickness of a piece of paper. That's a blink on the evolutionary time scale.

Fueled by a few SKYY vodka martinis, I began my own rant. The reason we haven't received signals from the intelligences in our galaxy, I surmised, is that they get just so far along and blow themselves up. The best we could do is leave a heap of fossils and some microcircuits that archaeologists from another planet would never figure out.

Intelligence is paper-thin on an evolutionary time scale and intrinsically self-destructive. I concluded my rant by surmising that the only life that will survive a global nuclear blowout are the radiation-hard cockroaches and the sharks, with their sophisticated nervous systems. They'll be the progenitors of nature's next experiment. We had our chance and blew it! My request of future generations is "prove me wrong."

Fight For Your Rights
with Other Inventors

In the 1980s, a wave of environmental lunacy gripped the New Jersey legislature. Due to the success of Tufoil, I had moved my factory to a larger facility. Suddenly we were faced with audits and hiring requirements, and we were forced to hire environmental advisors and lawyers to deal with problems that didn't exist. Arbitrariness tumbled on us. It infuriated me and, for the first time in my life, I became politically active. I discovered I wasn't alone. Howls of outrage from small business owners like myself emanated from all over the state. Enough was enough! I helped organize a group of like-minded souls— the Regulatory Reform Committee. It was there I met Bruce Siminoff, one of the few people I've met that I liked instantly.

Bruce was a partner in a very successful New Jersey-based venture capital and real estate development company. He was on numerous Boards of Directors and was active in community volunteer activities. When I met him he was the Director of the Commerce and Industry Association of NJ and Chairman of its State Issues Committee. I learned he had a profound knowledge of American history, was a Constitutional scholar, and the author of several books. He owned land in south Jersey and was constantly under attack by environmentalists. At the time, he was completing his book *Victim: Caught in the Environmental Web*, a well-documented record of the environmental obscenities coming from our legislature. In no time we became fast friends, much like two soldiers occupying a common foxhole on the battlefield. He was one of the most decent men I've ever met.

We attended endless meetings, gave countless testimonies in Trenton, and shared some very surreal situations. Once I was required to state my case before a committee of two in Trenton. One was a recent Rutgers graduate, the other a retired fireman, both clueless as to how environmental regulations were affecting businessmen. I handed them a photo I'd taken on my back porch depicting a friendly raccoon staring at me. I labeled the photo "Big Brother's Watching!"

Both appeared offended, but clearly, the intent was lost on both of them. I suspect neither of them had read

Orwell's *1984* or understood the depiction of Big Brother as an authoritarian government, organization or leader that exercises oppressive control over individuals. These two were just NJ Environmental Protection Agency puppets. I don't like to be shoved around, especially if I'm not guilty of any wrongdoing. The NJEPA, however, acted as if all developers and manufacturers were criminals against the planet. Their probing and questions reminded me of the Inquisition.

You Have to Mind the Store

My management philosophy is to hire people and let them loose. I'm a super delegator, not a micro-manager, because I want my employees to do what they do best, and I want to be free to do what I love most—invent. Sometimes that strategy backfires. I learned the hard way that if you're going to run a business, you have to know what's going on with every employee. As Reagan once said, "Trust, but validate." A business owner must trust employees but expect them to be accountable.

I've always considered my employees at Fluoramics to be like family. My wife and sons have worked there, and my secretary Paula has been with the company for thirty-five years. Even pets are welcome in the office. Knowing how I personally feel about a boss breathing down your neck, I respected my employees and gave them free reign to do what they did best, whether it was sales, marketing or plant management. I trusted my employees implicitly. It was always a sad day when an employee turned in a letter of resignation, for whatever reason.

In 1995, four employees resigned. The first to resign, in March, was our Sales Manager. She said she wanted to start a new career in the health profession. On her last day, we threw a party and gave her a $10,000 gift. Everyone kissed her and wished her well in her new profession. She sent heartfelt thank-you notes to all.

In June, one of our sales reps turned in his letter of resignation, saying he greatly appreciated the opportunity the Reick family afforded him to positively advance his professional career. Months earlier, he exhibited hostile behavior when the secretaries asked for his weekly itinerary. He wanted reimbursement for meals and hotels, but didn't want to say which customers he was visiting.

In July, I went on a scuba diving vacation in the Cayman Islands. The day I left, our Plant Manager resigned, saying he found a better-paying job doing warehouse work. And a few days later, one of our key distributors gave up his Tufoil distributorship. No explanation was offered.

A week later, we received our copies of *Road and Track* magazine and *Car and Driver* magazine. I noticed ads for products made by our distributor's company that sounded like ours! Could it be possible, I wondered, that our four employees had plotted to start a new company, using our technology, while collecting a paycheck and commissions from Fluoramics?

My son Gregg got hold of the desktop computer our sales rep had been using. We had purchased it for him; it was our property. But he had erased the hard drive. We called in a professional forensics firm that dealt with computer theft. Their technicians removed the hard drive from all the computers used by those employees and copied them onto another hard drive. We gave them keywords to search and they delivered the shocking evidence that our employees had been plotting for over a year, and among other things, had edited the word *Confidential* off our Formula-8 instructions. All our computer files with standing instructions had been accessed in one day as well.

They had developed a line of products that mirrored ours, in weeks! It had taken us eight years to come up with the correct formulae. We had a forensics expert from Rutgers do an analysis of the competing products, and his analysis was that their products were identical to ours. Clearly, they blatantly attempted to steal my company's proprietary information and use it to establish competing products!

We then went to the Automotive Aftermarket Products Expo (AAPEX) show, and the four miscreants were there as well, showing their full line of products. I went to the show's legal department, explained the situation, and showed them our attorney's brief. The lawyer read it, then confronted our former sales rep, the one who had refused to submit his itineraries. A hostile scene ensued.

In November, we were given a docket in the Bergen County Court, and sent a letter to our customers advising them of the legal action we were taking against our former employees, including the one who wrote this letter, after we'd given her a party and a $10,000 check: "I just wanted to say an extra thank you for giving me a lovely party today, as my last day. I really enjoyed the luncheon with everyone. I didn't think too much about leaving because if I did, I'd probably cry. I appreciate everything you did and I'm a better person for having met you. I will keep in touch. Have a good day!"

Looking back, I realized I mishandled many aspects of the legal case against these thieves. I was naive, but I had no reason to suspect that three of my most trusted employees—our Business Development Manager (4 years with Fluoramics), our Sales Manager (19 years!), and our Plant Manager (4 years)—as well as one of my top distributors, would steal our company's trade secrets, customer and prospect lists, and pricing and marketing strategies. They told our distributors and customers that Fluoramics was going out of business. To top it off, they planned their marketing strategies, designed labels and logos, and redirected Fluoramics phone and fax numbers to their new business while on Fluoramic's payroll! They lied about future employment plans to prevent me from discovering the conspiracy, and resigned while I was on vacation. What cowards! What *poseurs!* What frauds! It was the ultimate betrayal.

After $80,000 in attorney's fees and other expenses, I learned a great deal about our justice system, and that it doesn't favor small companies. Despite the egregious nature of their acts, they continued to market my products under a new name. While the courts did not find their actions criminal, I believe their disloyalty to be the greatest crime of all.

Dishonesty and betrayal are not uncommon in small businesses, I later learned. Sadly, most successful entrepreneurs have a similar story. Even sadder, in my case and others, is the perpetrators get away with it.

The best I can do is offer some suggestions on how to avoid this. In the years leading up to this outrage, I was being an inventor, working in my lab on the vapor phase creation of diamonds. This was a well-established science pioneered by the Russians. Volumes of literature exist, and I was trying to find a better way to grow the crystals. I had two electron microscopes in my lab to help me view the crystals I was growing.

My Sales Manager justified her betrayal by saying, "Frank is obsessed with his diamonds." I've always been obsessed with whatever I was working on—nothing new there. That's how I got into the New Jersey Inventors Hall of Fame and the Guinness Book of World Records. I had hired experts to market, sell and distribute Tufoil so I could be free to do what I love best—invent. Unfortunately, as a business owner, I wasn't minding the store, and I paid the price.

When You're Down and Out, Adopt a Fur Friend

A few months after the theft of our formulae, our beloved golden retriever Smiley died. Dogs have always been a part of my life, so I went to the local pound in search of a new dog companion. The operator of the place led me to a cage and introduced me to Brandy, a 2 ½ year-old golden retriever blend. I was told he suffered from separation anxiety, a euphemism for unmanageable. I went into the cage, sat on the floor, and looked Brandy in the eye. He put one paw on my knee as if to say, "Please pick me!" He was a clever chap and sized me up perfectly. He instinctively knew that I needed him as much as he needed me!

He was adopted into the Reick menagerie, which also included two partially feral cats. I've had Brandy five years, and we are inseparable. I take him to work every day, and he has free run of the woods surrounding the office. He still likes his ears rubbed, and likes to put his paw on my knee. We're a good team.

Have Fun and Be Adventurous

Besides supportive family, friends and pets, every inventor needs, (in addition to a laboratory where nobody can touch your pet projects), an adventurous hobby or diversion. I'm not one to get excited about watching football or basketball games on TV. Golf, gambling and gardening have never interested me. I'm too much of an animal lover to hunt, and hiking in the woods isn't my idea of an adventure, unless you encounter a bear. My boating days ended with my childhood canoe capers on Wappinger's Creek. What I love is flying and diving. I've owned a 1954 Vee Tail Bonanza N855 for years. Learning how to fly was an adult rite of passage that opened a whole new world to me.

My flying days go back to when I was at ITT. Many of my acquaintances there, bored or burned out by work, had taken flight lessons. Soon, flying was all they talked about. They encouraged me to take lessons, and so I did, with a flight instructor named Al Kolvites. In no time, I got my pilot's license. Al had a ritual when one of his students reached this milestone. He would take you up in a Cessna Aerobat with a roll of toilet paper. We'd fly up to about 5,000 feet, start a roll and throw the toilet paper out the window. We'd then turn the plane and chop the paper with the plane's propeller. It involved some steep turns (chandelles) and other wonderful maneuvers. It was mildly aerobatic. Chopping up toilet paper on my first flight as a bona fide pilot was a great rite of passage.

Like my friends, I loved the freedom of flying! I took my sons up, and gave them lessons. They loved it too! They all got their pilot's licenses, one before he got his driver's license.

After I'd been flying for a while, I had a burning desire to learn aerobatics—special maneuvers such as spins, loops and rolls. I'd had a little experience flying aerobatics, and that just whetted my appetite. Just north of Stewart Air Force Base in Newburgh, New York, there was an aerobatic flight school at the Cobelt Airport. I flew up there and introduced myself to the owner. He was an eccentric fellow who carried a .45 pistol in his belt. He pointed out all the small aerobatic planes, notably the Pitts Specials and the single-engine, two-seat Citabrias.

He also had a big Stearman, a biplane used to train pilots in WWII. The plane has a big radial engine out front, with wires and struts holding the wings together. It lands on two main wheels with a tail wheel—a three point landing. After the war, the planes were used as crop dusters, sports planes, and for aerobatic and wing walking in air shows.

The owner introduced me to my instructor, a thin, wiry, World War II fighter instructor. He was a colorful guy and swore a lot. While I was filling out the necessary paperwork, a Pitts Special came roaring down the runway, about ten feet off the ground, *upside down*. The Pitts Special is the *creme de la creme* of aerobatic aircraft and the most popular biplane used at air shows.

Cobelt Airport was a fun place to hang around. The people seemed just as crazy as the stunts they performed. I felt at home.

My instructor gave me a walk around the plane and explained all the dos and don'ts. To fly aerobatics, you must wear a parachute, he said. We put on our parachutes. We each wore a helmet with two earpieces and a long tube, a Gossport, that connected us. We then hopped into the airplane. He sat in the back seat, I sat in front.

Once we were strapped in, both seat belts and shoulder belts, a guy swung the propeller to get the engine going. Then my instructor shouted instructions into the Gossport. I did my best to understand him. It was rudimentary instruction, just like when I'd learned scuba diving: "Don't hold your breath on the way up kid!"

Once we were airborne, the flight was magnificent! If God had designed an airplane, it would have been the Stearman. It reminded me of the the ancient pterodactyl with a 40-foot wingspan. I followed his instructions as best as I could. He swore at me, shook his stick, and rolled the plane upside down. That's when I realized I did a couple of things wrong when I'd strapped myself in. I didn't pull the seat belt tight, and didn't have my feet under the pedal straps. So when we rolled, I was dangling upside down from the seat. Looking down at the ground, from 3,000 feet up, thoughts went through my mind, including, "Should I cut loose and parachute down?" I decided against that just as he rolled the plane right side up. I quickly pulled the seat belt tight, and stuck my feet under the pedal straps.

Then it was my turn to roll the plane. Securely fastened in, I took the time to look around and enjoy myself. The world looks so different from upside down. It was probably the most fun I've ever had in my life. When my son Kevin got his pilot's license, two weeks before his driver's license, I gave him an hour of Stearman time with the same flight instructor. He too had a marvelous time. Kudos to Mr. Stearman, who invented the plane.

Aerobatics may seem adventurous, but when it comes to flying, I'm a pilot who follows the rules. The basic rule is that when you're on the ground, you don't touch anything until you're off the runway. I don't hold any conversations on the ground and I say the following out loud three times: "Gear down speed. Propeller forward. Full

Rich. Air speed 90."

Even when you follow the drill precisely, you have to be prepared for unplanned disasters on the ground or in the air. And I've had my share! Once there was a bear on the runway just as I was about to take off! And on more than one occasion, my engine has gone dead in the air. Perhaps the most unnerving experience was when my son Gregg and I flew together to Wyoming to visit Bachman and his wife, who had retired there. As we approached Rapid City, South Dakota, I called flight control and requested a flight path over Mount Rushmore so we could view the presidential heads.

They replied, "Just don't go below 7,000 feet." Gregg already had his pilot's license and knew as well as I that you couldn't see anything from that elevation. As we approached the heads, the engine stopped. One thing that will get a pilot's attention in a hurry is the absence of engine noise.

We took a quick look at the instruments and noticed the exhaust gas temperature had shot up just before it went out. "Uh oh, we ran out of gas!" I groaned. I switched tanks, and the engine started up again. Whew! I called traffic control and told them I'd been on the wrong tank and apologized. It's happened twice since I've been flying. It's usually not a problem if you're at a high altitude, because you have time to figure out what's gone wrong. I now have five tanks and am very careful about my fuel levels.

As we got closer to Jackson Hole, we couldn't fly directly over the mountains because the maximum altitude for my plane is 13,000 feet. The mountains around Jackson Hole are 14,000 feet; the Jackson Hole Airport is 8,000 feet. We flew into North Valley, and had problems there as well, this time with landing. A wind came in over the Grand Tetons, looped down into the Valley and then back up again. The plane didn't want to descend; an updraft was keeping it up, despite the fact that the gear and flaps were down. Eventually, with racing hearts and sweaty palms, we landed, and kissed the ground.

Besides flying and aerobatics, I love diving. I'd been hard-hat diving for a decade before I went scuba diving off Marathon Key in Florida, back in the sixties. I was visiting my mother in Bradenton, Florida, where she had retired. I borrowed her car and drove to Marathon Key, where an ex-patriot named Matthew Ferguson ran a dive shop. We got to talking about diving, and he offered to take me out onto the reef. He put several tanks of air in his aluminum boat, and we motored out to the reef. I'd never used an aqualung before, but had read about them in Cousteau's book *Silent World*.

We passed a lighthouse on the reef manned by two Coast Guard men. To pass time, they climbed to the top of the lighthouse and free-dived sixty foot deep. Matthew told me that was all they did all day—climb, dive, and swim. They were in great shape. I'd stayed in good shape since my summer working at the cement plant, and could free-dive to sixty feet. But I looked like a wimp next to those guys.

Nowadays, to scuba dive, you have to take all kinds of certifications, but back then, Matthew gave me just a few words of advice: "There's a pull bar on the side. When you can't breathe easily, it will give you extra air. Don't hold your breath on the way up or you'll rupture your lungs. Follow your bubbles up."

I donned the scuba tank, mask and fins, and tumbled over the side of the boat. I dove down about thirty-five feet; the visibility was about a hundred feet. The reef was pristine, populated by great mounds of colorful corals, waving sea fans, and schools of tropical fish—parrot fish, angel fish and barracudas. It was spectacular! And noisy! An active undersea world of wonder. I've done a lot of diving since then, but nothing has come close to the beauty of that reef.

I revisited it years later, hoping to share the beauty with my oldest son Kevin. We didn't use tanks, just did free-diving. The coral was bleached out and silted over. Sea grass had taken over most of the flat areas. Very few fish remained. What a man-made disaster!

Even though Kevin was a little kid, still in grade school, he was an excellent swimmer. He was determined to keep up with me while I was free diving, despite the fact that his ears hurt. I had taught him how to pop his ears, but he didn't do it correctly. As a result, he ruptured an eardrum, which didn't heal properly. Then he spent weeks in the hospital to repair his ears. Ever since that incident, he's been reluctant to do any free-diving.

I raised my three boys rough and tumble. Like me, they were little Huck Finns. In our backyard we built log cabins and tree forts. We went camping, boating, hiking, flying, and diving. I hung Tarzan swings from trees for them to swing on. We did a lot of dangerous things. Danger never worried me. I strongly believe that danger hones your skills and you have to expose yourself to controlled danger. But from that diving incident with my young son, I learned to respect the limitations of anyone following you.

Use Your first Amendment Rights

In 1970, when I was inducted into the New Jersey Inventors Hall of Fame for work I had done on superconductivity, I told the audience a story that Bob Adams had told me years ago, when he was working in my dad's jewelry store and we were both inventing perpetual motion machines. The story took place on a sloping hill above the Hudson, where a group of people was staring down at an odd-looking boat with a pipe stack on top. The people chanted in unison, "He'll never get it to work! He'll never get it to work!" Moments later, there was a clank and a bang from inside the boat, smoke came out the funnel, and the boat started moving upriver. The chanting suddenly changed to "He'll never get it to stop! He'll never get it to stop!"

Inventors face a world of critics. More often than not, the critics prefer to dismiss or tear down our ideas rather than see how a new or improved product can impact the world. These critics are often brilliant people, but they lack imagination. Or they're just arrogant.

This story reminded me of a talk I was invited to give to a group of corporate executives at a major automobile company in Detroit. I was picked up in a stretch limo by the Director of Research, a nice enough guy, who later introduced me to a dozen or so engineers. I recognized many around the table, as we belong to the same scientific societies. I spoke about Tufoil, my lubricant that got into the Guinness Book of Records, one that could prolong the life of automobiles. It was available for sale in retail stores nationwide and doing well. The engineers seemed interested. I rode back to the airport with the Research Director. En route, he looked me straight in the eye and said, "Frank, we make cars to last 100,000 miles." That was before the Japanese taught Detroit automakers how to make cars. His statement showed the arrogance of large corporations. While flying my plane back to New Jersey, I made a decision to not deal with large, bureaucratic corporations that were "set in their old ways."

Like most inventors, I'm an optimist, and I want my grandchildren to have the same opportunities I had. I want to believe that every member of our society wants to study in school, work hard to better themselves, to ultimately be productive members of society, and to take personal responsibility for the choices they make. That's the credo we inventors live by. But not all do, I've found, in my eight decades.

I see trends in our country and around the world that

I find troubling and unsettling. And I'm not alone. In any gathering of inventors, whether two or twenty, our conversations are often about the unbridled growth and incompetence of government, and the negative consequences for free markets, free thinkers, free society... and inventors and entrepreneurs.

Although the opinions that follow are mine, they reflect the feelings of many of my fellow inventors.

I'm appalled at the economic illiteracy of politicians in both political parties. I never studied economics or law in college, but common sense tells me the government has turned its back on the Constitution and pursued the same policies that caused the American colonists to revolt against the British Crown more than 225 years ago. Have these politicians and bureaucrats no sense of history? Are they so intent on getting elected and re-elected, to hang onto their perks of office, that they don't give a damn about the future of the country? Congress has become a privileged class subject to different rules than We the People.

On my office wall I have a million peso note from Argentina and a 20 million German Mark dated 1923 as a reminder of how central banks devalue a nation's currency by printing more money. The new money is used to buy a national government's debt because the budget deficit is out of sight. Sound familiar? That's what the Federal Reserve has been doing to our country. They've printed trillions of dollars to bailout Wall Street, the banking system, General Motors, AIG, Fannie Mae and

Freddie Mac. Santayana said "those who don't remember the past are condemned to repeat it."

No good comes from printing money. True wealth comes from creativity and production, not printing money. If creating money is the panacea to a nation's economic ills, then why didn't Argentina prosper after its central bank created untold billions of pesos? And how about Germany in the 1930s? Printing money, and war, is dangerous for a nation. Ernest Hemingway once observed, "The first panacea for a mismanaged nation is inflation of the currency; the second is war. Both bring a temporary prosperity; both bring permanent ruin. But both are the refuge of political and economic opportunists."

In my opinion, the lowest forms of humanity on the planet are the opportunists and con artists who produce nothing, create nothing, and bully those who do. These bullies make life miserable for people who just want to lead productive lives, free of the tentacles of an oppressive government. I am talking about the political class in our society, the self-serving parasites that have created the financial mess our country is in today, after decades of promising that a "Great Society" would be created by taxing, spending, borrowing and printing money. Needless to say, their multi-year experiment has failed. The Federal Government is bankrupt. The Federal Reserve's printing press continues to bail out the government's unsustainable spending and endless wars overseas, and has postponed the "day of reckoning."

Have we not learned from the great statesman Cicero, who in 55 B.C. proclaimed, "The budget should be balanced, the Treasury should be refilled, public debt should be reduced, the arrogance of officialdom should be tempered and controlled, and the assistance to foreign lands should be curtailed, lest Rome become bankrupt. People must again learn to work instead of living on public assistance."

Just as scary as the ignorance of the political class is the domination of "crony capitalism" in America. Crony capitalism, also known as corporate welfare, exists when a particular business gets favors from politicians in the form of tax breaks, legal permits, government grants, direct government subsidies, and government bailouts. Examples that come to mind are GE and NBC, as well as several "green energy" companies such as Solyndra.

Crony capitalism goes against the ideas of free enterprise and limited government. As a small business owner, I practice what's known as *laissez faire* capitalism. I rely on my inventions and ability to market products that are the result of my discoveries to make a living. I don't want or get government assistance to create or sell my products in the marketplace. If I fail, I don't get a government bailout. If I succeed, the federal government exacts its pound of flesh in the form of taxes.

Crony capitalists want the benefits of free enterprise but not the risks. Crony capitalists and their political puppets have been ruling America since Alexander Hamilton, the country's first Secretary of the Treasury, who established the first centralized Bank of the United States. Books by economist Thomas DiLorenzo, historian Thomas Woods, and so many others, reveal how America has become a crony capitalist society. As more Americans realize we have been conned by politicians who have promised "bread and circuses" since the beginning of the republic, the crony capitalists and their defenders in DC are very worried. Now that the well has nearly run dry to maintain the welfare state, the crony capitalists will have to regroup with their bought puppets to pull off more egregious policies to keep the con alive.

Like many of my fellow inventors, I'm often appalled by the seeming mindlessness of our government. A case in point is their phasing out of LORAN, a long range navigation system developed after World War II. LORAN, which enabled ships and aircraft determine their speed and location, was based on huge antennae farms and low frequency signals. It's a rugged, dependable system that worked well. It isn't dependent of the view of the sky, on micro circuits or signals from outer space. I depended on it when I was flying my plane.

Recently I was flying my plane and the LORAN system kept sending error signals. When I got home, I went on the Internet and learned it had been disabled by the government in 2010. Instead, they're putting all their eggs in the satellite-based GPS (Global Positioning System) basket. I'm personally annoyed because I have one in my airplane that doesn't work now. More important is the potential harm to our country by being increasingly dependent on satellites and GPS. A technologically savvy dictator could set off an atomic bomb in outer space which will throw out an electromagnetic pulse (EMP) that will fry every microcircuit on the planet. When the satellite-based GPS system is deactivated by this, aircraft and cars will wonder where they are because there won't be any navigation signals to pick up.

This type of disaster scenario wouldn't affect the LORAN system, because the EMP would have no effect on it. For the government to rely on one system without a reasonable backup is an invitation for disaster. The question is not if it's going to happen, but how soon.

I'm concerned about the number of Americans who embrace the redistribution of wealth philosophy, also known as "robbing Peter to pay Paul." President Kennedy's famous words "Ask not what your country can do for you, but what you can do for your country" have been reversed. The most Googled words are "how to get free ..." with the "..." being food stamps, daycare, housing, and college education. In their seeking of these free goods and services, they've embraced the lies of politicians. To believe there's an easy path in life, financed by the government, is a Faustian bargain. Selling your soul for what appears to be cradle to grave subsistence is an illusion. This belief in redistribution of wealth only breeds an amoral society.

Politicians are good at what they do—getting elected. But what have they done in DC for all these years except perpetuate the failed welfare state that keeps people dependent on money that has been plundered from fellow citizens? The more I hear politicians, from both political parties, talk about the "poor and underprivileged" I want to ask them what they have done to create businesses to eradicate this class?

They will point to all the government programs to help small businesses and the economy in general. Nonsense! Government subsidies may help a business get financing, but where does the money come from? For every government "action" to help a business, there is a real "reaction" in that one or more businesses will not get funded. Frederic Bastiat, the French economist, philosopher, attorney and member of the legislature observed, more than 150 years ago, that every time government does something supposedly for the good of the economy, "the seen," we have to remember the bad that occurs, namely, "the unseen," what was lost, not produced or created by individuals who had to pay the taxes to pay for government programs.

Bastiat, the originator of the classic "broken window fallacy," demolished the proposition that government largesse or destruction, in the case of the boy who breaks a shopkeeper's window, is good news to the glazier. The glazier has more business due to the broken window. While the glazier benefits from the destruction of the window, the shopkeeper now cannot buy a suit, so the tailor is the loser. By the same token, government redistribution of resources benefits someone at the expense of others in society.

I'm also appalled at corruption in our legal system, especially one that let the four miscreants who conspired to steal my company's products in 2005 blatantly get away with it. I have nothing more to say about this.

Live With Gratitude

There's only one country in the world, and perhaps in the history of mankind, where a person like me could do what I love for most of my life. During the past six decades I learned to fly a plane, started several companies, was awarded dozens of patents, chose challenging and interesting projects to work on, and was recognized for my talents in the laboratory by the Guinness Book of World Records and the New Jersey Inventor's Hall of Fame. During my life, I've fraternized with fascinating inventors, worked with dedicated and skilled employees, and have had numerous faithful and loving animal companions. Most important is that my wife and I are blessed to have two intelligent and successful sons who are also pilots, and three wonderful and talented granddaughters.

I've told you my story, of the forces in play that led me down the path of becoming an inventor. My story isn't a cookie cutter pattern for all inventors. We all come from different circumstances, and have all had various degrees of financial success. But we are united by a desire to create and make products that enhance the living standard for all people.

I feel such gratitude to the many male influences/mentors who stepped up to the plate after my father died in 1944, when I was fourteen. Dad meant the world to me, and I so admired his skills, tenacity and kindness. I was so fortunate to have him as my father, and I often hear his encouraging voice, "You can do it, Frank." I wish every young man and woman could have mentors.

At fourteen, I was smart, but also a smart aleck, and my life could easily have taken a wrong turn if these men—Bob Adams, Mr. Archibald, Mr. Bigelow, Mr. Hawkins and Dr. Bachman, hadn't taken me under their wings. Like Dad, they were hard-working, productive members of society who believed you could achieve anything you set your mind to. They made sure I channeled my intellect, energy and insatiable curiosity toward math and science, which paved the way for me to become an inventor. They all knew just the right words to motivate me. "Keep working, Frank" and "You can do better, Frank." They are the Fathers of my inventions.

As an inventor, I was fortunate to have met my patent attorney Mike Ebert, who introduced me to his stable of inventors, some of whom I collaborated with over the years, and sustained friendships with over four decades: Maurice Kanbar, Dr. Joe Wilder, George Castanis, and Bruce Siminoff among them.

There have been low points as well. One is too painful to write about, the loss of a son in the prime of his life. There is no greater loss.

Declaring bankruptcy after a failed business venture was a huge psychological and emotional blow. From that experience, however, I learned it wasn't the end of the world, just an opportunity to start anew with a different perspective on life. Failure taught me to focus on what I loved to do, inventing. If I become fabulously wealthy in the process, great! But if riches decreased my motivation to invent, or if concern for my worldly goods and investments took time away from inventing, I'd rather be inventing.

At age 82, my latest invention is a solvent-free lubricant and rust inhibitor called HinderRUST. Like all my other products, it comes with a story. I was driving my car one day, hit the brake pedal, and it went all the way to the floor! As a pilot trained to handle such situations, I was able to maneuver the car to safety without incident. Once I got the car to the repair shop, I learned that the metal brake lines had rusted through. In my usual take charge way, I vowed to find a solution.

I thought it was absolutely unforgivable that the auto manufacturer would build a time bomb like that into a car. I said to myself, 'I've got to do something about this." That got me interested in rust. And I spent my late seventies doing research on rust chemistry. My goals in developing HinderRUST were: First — no solvents. Two — it had to be a good lubricant. Third — it had to be the best rust inhibitor in the world. It got so good, we found out that we had jumped way ahead of the pack. It's a product that can make anything made of metal last longer! Now I need to invent a product that will make humans immortal.

That brings me to the subject of retirement. I'm often asked when I'm going to retire. My reply is, "I've been retired for the past fifty years!" Seriously, I'm having too much fun at Fluoramics to retire. *Every day is a vacation!* My secretary Paula Douglas, who has been with the company for 35 years, takes care of all the important paperwork required to run a business. My production manager, Sederick Nelson, handles all production in the factory. Brandy comes to work with me every day.

For me, retirement would be a certain death sentence. I don't consider myself a workaholic or a driven man. I just have fun at what I do. What keeps you alive is looking over the horizon, like a dog hanging his head out the window of a car and thinking, "Oh boy! What are we going to do next?"

My factory is filled with symbols from my life—it's a museum of sorts—to remind me of where I've been, where I still want to go, and the lessons I've learned. In one corner I have a bent propeller from a bad landing that resulted in $20K in damage. It kept my plane out of action for a year, but I survived. I have a statue of Icarus in another corner to remind me to keep my wings glued on properly. I have a snorkel that reminds me of my diving days. On it is a sign that says "For Emergency Use Only—When the BS Gets Too High." That's what I point to when so-called "authorities," con men, and BS artists visit me. I have a stuffed toy rat to remind me of when I was bit by a rat as a child, and later, metaphorically, as an adult. I have favorite quotes about inventions hanging on the walls. One of my favorites is this one, conceived by my secretary Paula: "Always do your last experiment first."

The concept of role models and mentoring continues to be important to me. I mentored my sons and many of their friends. When they were young, we did algebra and word problems together. I wanted them to have fun with problems, not recoil from them. When the boys were in grade school and their friends came into my lab, I gave them a pile of junk to play with, just as Dad and "Uncle Bob" had done with me. When they were teens, I built computers with them and showed them how to fix cars. When we were testing Tufoil, my front yard resembled an auto junkyard. I taught my boys how to fly at a young age and we often took trips together. I taught them lessons about money and explained why I never bought anything new in my life. Instead, I showed them how to repair and resurrect items left for dead.

I've been a mentor to dozens of aspiring entrepreneurs/inventors. For twenty years, I've been on the Board of Directors for the Foundation for Free Enterprise. I speak to business students as often as I can on campuses. I tell them I've never borrowed a nickel in my life (and it's not because I inherited it!). I never took out a small business loan and I never had a business plan. I know that goes against all the advice given to startup businesses: Business plan! Business plan! Business plan! I didn't hire a fancy PR agency either. I read the Ogilvy book on public relations and advertising, and we did all our ads and PR in-house. As Frank Sinatra crooned, "I did it my way."

One lesson I've learned from Dad's untimely death and the deaths of my closest friends, is that it's important at my age to stay in shape. Fifteen years ago I had asymptomatic cardiac fibrillation and my doctor installed a pacemaker. I couldn't fly for a year after that; a flight surgeon had to sign off on that. For now, I fly one hour a week, to keep both me and my plane from getting rusty. I've gotten in the habit of swimming every night and walking on the treadmill. At work, I'm on my feet all day, walking around the building. And I take walks with my dog Brandy.

I compare my life to Voltaire's Candide, who goes through one disaster after another, but dusts himself off and continues on to face another exciting adventure. That's what has made me happy. Life, after all, is supposed to be fun.

At 82, I believe my soul is immortal. I also believe in reincarnation and hope I come back as a magnificent flying creature—preferably a hawk—which I'm convinced are reincarnated pilots. The human experience is nature thinking about itself, talking about and observing what a marvelous, magical thing we are because we don't understand it. Who cares? Every year becomes more mysterious; 300 new planets were discovered last year. How many marvelous man-made inventions will be produced?

POSTSCRIPT

My father, friends, and mentors who have passed on are immortal because of their ideas, inspirational thoughts, and their inventions that have outlived their physical bodies. I conclude this memoir with a final tribute to them.

Dr. Charles Bachman

Although we no longer worked together after our entrepreneurial adventure, Dr. Bachman and I stayed close. While he was still teaching, he and his wife took an annual summer vacation overseas. Florence and I often house-sat for them at their house in Jamesville, New York, just south of Syracuse. The house was constructed of cinder blocks and concrete atop a Drummlin glacial hill—gravel and rock deposited by a glacier 10,000 years earlier. He had built it with the help of his Physics students; all got As that year.

His library was exquisite, and within it, he had a tape recorder with big six-inch reels. He recorded classical music off the New York City radio station WQXR. One one occasion, I put on a tape while working in the laboratory. Hearing Beethoven's Concerto No. 5, *The Emperor*, reverberating as if I was in a cathedral, was a magnificent experience.

I was also a voracious reader, and took advantage of his library. I read everything written by Dostoevsky and Emerson, and absorbed their ideas like a sponge. I was going through H.G. Wells' *Outline of History* and became fascinated with the life of Gautama Siddhattah Buddha. I was looking for a philosophy to live by, and though raised a Methodist, I was more drawn to Buddhism than Christianity. The concept of nirvana intrigued me.

Bachman frequently visited India. He had a Fulbright Scholarship, and spent time teaching there. Aware of my interest in the teachings of Buddha, Bachman purchased a two-foot tall brass statue of a seated Buddha on one of his trips, boxed it up, and sent it to me. After opening it, I noticed something was rattling around inside. I removed the bottom and discovered a piece of cloth and some sticks. Not knowing these were sacred mantra rolls, placed there after the statue had been consecrated by a monk, I threw them out, learning later that I'd greatly reduced the spiritual value of the statue. Despite this, it has resided in my bedroom since then—very peaceful.

Bachman and his wife spent their last years in a log cabin he built near Jackson Hole, Wyoming. One summer, my son Gregg and I flew out in my V-Tail Bonanza to visit them. I wanted him to meet them, especially since

Bachman had been my mentor and surrogate father, and had had a profound influence on my life.

We spent several days visiting with them. One night, while Bachman and I were sitting outside reminiscing, I told him how important he had been in my life, that I was grateful that he took an interest in me, and that he saw something in me that nobody else did. Tears came to his eyes and his voice cracked. "Frank" he whispered, "I hoped I had some influence on some of my students."

I never forgot that. He was the most lucid physics teacher I'd ever met. I loved his classes and I loved being in his presence. He'd spent his whole life teaching, and at this stage of his life, he was questioning if it was the right thing to do.

Bachman died at the age of 95. He was addicted to peanut butter. A nurse friend once told me, "That stuff will kill you sooner or later."

Mike Ebert

Mike Ebert, my patent attorney, eventually retired and moved to Israel. Soon after, he was diagnosed with malignant melanoma, which originated from a mole on his back. After he was diagnosed, he visited the U.S. He called me from the city and said, "Frank, I'd like to come out and have a talk." I assumed he was going to drive out to my plant in Mahwah, but he'd taken the bus from the city! He looked much older but his intellectual curiosity hadn't waned. We talked for four hours, and hadn't scratched the surface of topics in which we shared interests. I didn't realize the gravity of his diagnosis, and assumed we'd see each other again. He passed away soon after our visit. Only then did I realize he'd come to say goodbye. I'm sure I wasn't the only member of Mike's flock that broke down when I heard the news. His clients were creative visionaries, but Mike's star showed them the way. He was a living legend.

Bruce Siminoff

I've never met a man more passionate about liberty than Bruce. He was a warrior for the cause, but instead of fighting overseas, he fought his battles at home. He wrote books, articles and lectured all over the country about the mindless environmental regulation that destroyed individuals and businesses. With his keen mind and ability to organize, (he was the Director of the NJ Commerce and Industry Association for many years), he would have made a fine Governor or President. He also loved to fly, taught me how to invest in the stock market, and helped me write the book "Flying the Stock Market."

Bruce died of a brain tumor in 2008. His legacy is two books on liberty: *The Liberty Crisis* and *Victim: Caught in the Environmental Web*, his testimonies in Trenton, as well as numerous published articles on environmental regulation. The cause for liberty is stronger than ever in the U.S.

Doug Scharp

Doug and I lost touch after I'd left ITT Nutley, but one day, years later, I got a phone call from him. "Frank," he said, in a raspy voice, "I just had one lung removed and the doc said I'm gonna be dead in six months." When we had worked together, the only issue we disagreed on was his smoking. He smoked cigarettes until all that was left was a stub. I hadn't smoked since my teen years, and had warned him against it, for health reasons. He didn't heed my advice. He loved to smoke! True to the doctor's prediction, he did die of lung cancer. I couldn't bring myself to attend his funeral. I knew I would break down and sob, just like I had at my father's funeral. To this day I regret my decision to not pay my respects to a man I so revered.

Bob Adams

I lost track of "Uncle Bob" after I had left for college in 1948. In 1949, Mother sold the jewelry store after I showed no interest in running it. She also sold the barn Dad had built to "Uncle Bob," who converted it into his home. He'd lost interest in his house on the rock hill and had never finished blasting the rock for a basement. He didn't finish the violin he was making either. He went from one interest to another, it seemed. He was like Dad, who also lost interest in things too. Once the barn was built, he never used it for anything but storage. And he never farmed the land around it. Developers eventually bought the property and built nice houses.

Twenty years later, while working at ITT, I sought out Bob. I found him back in Poughkeepsie, running a soft ice cream store near his home on Wappinger's Creek.

I dropped in one day, and found him cleaning the ice cream machine. At first he didn't recognize me; I had to tell him who I was. We chit-chatted about the past. He had changed, but so had I. During my visit a couple of kids came in and they called him "Uncle Bob" too. He treated them the same way he had treated me when I was younger. It wasn't until then that I realized he was "Uncle" Bob to lots of kids; always being a mentor of sorts.

I didn't visit him again until several years later, when I was learning to fly and had landed in Poughkeepsie. He had retired and was living in a rest home. I barely recognized him. He was old and feeble and could barely keep up with the conversation. I reminded him of the Sunday mornings when I visited him and his wife on Cherry Street. He said, "You know, Frank, I had God-awful hangovers on those mornings." Only then did I learn that the merchants on Main Street, including my father, used to buy a bottle of whiskey on Saturday nights and convene in Bob's store, discussing their dreams and aspirations, asking "What if?" questions, and anticipating "Ah HA!" moments.

Wappinger's Creek

In 2010 I visited Poughkeepsie and Wappinger's Creek to retrace the footsteps of my youth. My former homes, and earliest labs, were either torn down or in a state of disrepair. Bob Adams' store was covered in graffiti. I visited the Adams' home on the slate rock, and chatted with the new owner. She didn't know much about the history of the area, so I filled her in. The basement was still a rubble of rocks, unchanged since Bob decided to stop blasting and build a violin instead.

I visited the area where Dad had built his barn. The barn was gone, replaced by a stately home with a sunken pool in back. The owner told me he didn't let his kids play in the woods due to deer ticks and Lyme disease. He also said he and his wife felt the place was haunted; they often sensed a harmless presence. I wondered if it might be Dad, or Bob Adams, but then recalled once briefly seeing my deceased mother sitting in the backseat of my plane!

I checked the area of the creek in front of my father's cabin. The open fields I remembered had been replaced by mature trees. The water behind the Wappinger's Creek dam was more like a muddy stream than a lake and the dam appeared on the verge of collapse. No signs of frogs, turtles, fish or wild birds in sight. Muddy banks replaced the verdant slope that had once been lined with iris. The magic that had inspired me as a young boy was gone.

By Franklin G. Reick

ARTICLES

"Flying the Stock Market: Pilot Your Dollars to Success", by Franklin G. Reick and Bruce G. Siminoff (Author), Glenbridge Publishing (January 1997).

"Nobody's That Stupid," *Bonanza Society Bulletin* (he was prompted to writing the article after landing his Bonanza at Ramapo Valley Airport, with the landing gear retracted.)

"Low Temperature Signal Detection in Optically Pumped Rubidium Vapor", published in *Journal of Applied Physics*, November 1970.

"The Optical Whispering Mode of Polished Cylinders and Its Implication in Laser Technology": published in *Applied Optics*, November 1965.

"Through a Glass Brightly", published in *Electronics*, February 5, 1968.

"Stable PTFE Colloids as Lubricating Oil Additives", published as a series in *American Laboratory Magazine*—Part 1, June 1977; Part 2, March 1978.

"Energy-Saving Lubricants", published in *Lubrication Engineering*, Volume 38, 10, 635-646, May 1981.

"Intensity Distribution of Light Leaving a Hemicylinder", published in *Proceedings of the Symposium on Quasi-Optics*, Polytechnic Institute of Brooklyn, June 1964.

"Relevances in Material Science and Application of High Temperature Superconductors", *AMSAHTS '90*, NASA *Conference Publications 10043*, 1990, "Plastic Superconductor Bearings (Any shape), 77K and Up" (p. 435) with Dr. Larry Bennett.

"The Graded Boundary Electrode", Invited paper, Electrochemical Society, Boston 1962.

UNITED STATES PATENTS

Patent Number 5,339,061
An iron-free transformer

Patent Number 5,180,706
High-temperature porous-ceramic superconductor

Patent Number 4,999,322
High-temperature porous-ceramic superconductor
U.S. Patent Number 4,606,735
Medical tubing holder

Patent Number 4,605,990
Surgical clip-on light pipe illumination assembly

Patent Number 4,562,832
Medical instrument and light pipe illumination assembly

Patent Number 4,525,286
Enhanced grease

Patent Number 4,465,058
Solar energy air-heating system

Patent Number 4,421,658
Halocarbon-soluble molybdenum composition

Patent Number 4,377,166
Surgical evacuator

Patent Number 4,349,444
Hybrid PTFE lubricant including molybdenum compound

Patent Number 4,333,840
Hybrid PTFE lubricant for weapons

Patent Number 4,284,519
Halocarbon oil composition

Patent Number 4,284,518
Stabilized hybrid lubricant

Patent Number 4,224,173
Lubricant oil containing polytetrafluorethylene and fluorochemical surfactant

Patent Number 4,199,142
Toys and games using super-hydrophobic effects

Patent Number 4,172,724
Water maze game with super-hydrophobic surface

Patent Number 4,127,491
Hybrid lubricant including halocarbon oil

Patent Number 4,085,365
Earphone adapter for aircraft radios

Patent Number 4,059,018
Direct-acting low-pressure sensor

Patent Number 4,053,443
Sealing compound

Patent Number 3,976,572
Aircraft fuel contaminant tester

Patent Number 3,933,656
Lubricating oil with fluorocarbon additive

Patent Number 3,931,428
Substrate coated with super-hydrophobic layers.

Patent Number 2,899,532
Electrode wick

Patent Number 3,027,278
Carbon Coating

Patent Number 3,026,572
Candle Molding

Patent Number 3,615,985
Tubeless Tire Repair Plug insertion technique

Patent Number 3,638,644
Illuminated Appliance

Patent Number 3,641,332
Fiber Optics Illumination System

Patent Number 3,799,832
Technique for Bonding Tetrafluoroethylene Sheet to
    Metal Substrate

Patent Number 3,879,302
Fluorocarbon-based Sealing Compound

Patent Number 3,914,802
Non-Thrombogenic Prosthetic Material

COMPANIES FORMED

Diversified Technology, Inc.
World Craft Inc.
Fluoramics Inc.
Westwood Aero Labs Inc.
Bald Eagle Holdings Inc.
Briareos Inc
HinderRust Inc.

WEBSITES

www.tufoil.com
www.fluoramics.com
www.sskiwax.com
www.hinderrust.com

Our ad campaign for Tufoil featured animal stories. To read them, visit:
http://www.fluoramics.com/animal_stories.shtml

Follow us on Facebook, YouTube, Twitter and Google-Plus.

To reach us, write to:
Fluoramics, Inc.
18 Industrial Avenue
Mahwah, NJ 07430
or call 800-922-0075

www.ingramcontent.com/pod-product-compliance
Lightning Source LLC
LaVergne TN
LVHW091256080426
835510LV00007B/285